SARAH BROWN'S

HEALTHY

PREGNANCY

A VEGETARIAN APPROACH

BBC BOOKS

Sarah Brown is a household name in vegetarian cookery. Her previous books include *Vegetarian Kitchen*, *The New Vegetarian Kitchen*, *Quick and Easy Vegetarian Cookery*, and the walking book *Sarah Brown's Secret England*, which reflects her enthusiasm for a healthy lifestyle. She had her first baby, Ralph, in 1990 and mother and son are a shining example of the merits of a vegetarian diet. Sarah Brown lives in Richmond, Surrey.

Published by BBC Books,
a division of BBC Enterprises Limited,
Woodlands, 80 Wood Lane, London W12 0TT

First published 1992

© Sarah Elizabeth Brown Limited 1992

ISBN 0 563 36248 0

Exercise illustrations by Penny Sobr
Other illustrations by Sandra Pond and Will Giles
Photoset in 10/11 Sabon by Redwood Press Limited
Printed and bound in Great Britain by Clays Ltd, St Ives plc
Cover printed by Clays Ltd, St Ives plc

Contents

Acknowledgements

Many people have helped me in the course of writing this book, not least the staff at University College Hospital, London who delivered Ralph safely and who gave us both such excellent postnatal care. I would also like to thank my NCT teacher, Lyn Thompson, for her invaluable antenatal classes and my breast feeding counsellor, Meg Walker, for all her advice and interest in this project. My thanks also go to Jocelyn Taylor for her role as our health visitor and for her useful comments on the manuscript. Dr Joyce Woffindin and her husband Dr Peter Hemingway, in spite of their busy professional lives found time to read the manuscript and made many helpful remarks – my thanks to them.

I am grateful to all those who discussed various alternative therapies with me including Suzanne Adamson, Julian Barnard, Susan Curtis, Steve Jones, Beverley Muir, Susan Pready and Lolly Stirk.

Encouragement from BBC Enterprises was a great help to me especially as the deadline approached, and I would like to thank Heather Holden-Brown and Anna Ottewill for their enthusiasm for this book.

Above all, special thanks to my husband Paul Street for his interest, involvement and unfailing support.

This book has no special dedication but I would like to mention both my parents, Lewis and Elizabeth Brown, and Paul's parents, Brian and Sheila Street. Now we too are parents, we have a better understanding of all the hard work that goes into bringing up children. The start of this book seems a good place to say thank you.

Introduction

I have written this book to reassure anyone who is hoping to become pregnant, or indeed anyone who already is pregnant, that a vegetarian diet is a very good diet. It is not only more than adequate in pregnancy but in many ways can be positively beneficial. I found it very inspiring that good nutrition and healthy eating could contribute so much to your own well being as well as giving your baby a good start.

My own baby Ralph was virtually a New Year present. It was on the last day of December that I first thought it was possible that I might be pregnant. We dutifully had a very sober celebration to welcome 1990. All I could think of was rushing out as soon as possible to get a DIY pregnancy kit and see if lack of a period and slightly swollen breasts meant something. As soon as this showed positive, I was off to the doctor, feeling very thrilled and very special. I was just a little deflated when I was told, very kindly, that this was very early days. Her advice was to wait for at least a fortnight and make another appointment. Then we could talk about hospitals, dates of delivery and so on. A fortnight! It seemed an age. It also began to dawn on me that if fourteen days seemed a long time to wait, how would the next eight months feel? Time to put things in perspective.

That fortnight did pass, of course, as did the next eight months or so. Ralph was born on 10 September at University College Hospital, London. He weighed 4.3 kg (9^1/$_2$ lb).

You will see that I have used the pronoun 'he' whenever I refer to the baby or prospective baby. That is because for me 'it' was a 'he'. No bias is intended.

Looking back, I enjoyed my pregnancy and my son's first year enormously. It was a wonderful learning experience both in the first stage when there is so much to discover as your own body changes, then, after the birth, as a parent. Motherhood is hard work but it is constantly rewarding as you watch your baby discover the world around him. There are so many milestones in that first year. His first smile, his recognition of you, his first spoonful of food, and perhaps that first tentative step all by himself.

Every mother wants the best for herself and her new born child. In wanting the best, you also want to be sure your diet is as good as it can be. Whilst being conscious of the general benefits of a vegetarian diet, once planning to be pregnant I thought it was a good time to look closely at my diet. I'd lived happily and healthily without meat and fish for nearly fifteen years, but was I eating well enough to cope with the demands of pregnancy? Would the diet provide me with the extra calcium and iron needed? Would it help me to overcome some of the common complaints of pregnancy such as constipation? This book focuses on how to get the best from a meat- and fish-free diet, but many of the suggestions and ideas I've given will help anyone who is interested in being healthy during pregnancy.

Whether you are healthy during pregnancy won't be entirely a matter of your diet. It is as well to be fit overall, and I've suggested some exercise routines (and relaxation ideas) to help you.

For many people reading this book, pregnancy will be an entirely new experience. It certainly helps to understand a little of what is likely to happen to you over the next nine months or so, as this puts the nutritional advice in context. I've given a broad outline of the various stages of pregnancy including what you may feel and what happens to you and the growing baby. There is also a description of labour and some advice as to how to recover once you have had your baby. Vegetarians don't always find food in hospitals ideal so there are also some suggestions as to how to cope there.

The great joy of pregnancy is that when it comes to an end there is a new beginning. Once you have had your baby, there is the question of feeding him. Initially there is the decision whether to breast or bottle feed. When you begin introducing solid food there is the question of making sure your child has the right nutrients. In this book, I've written about food during the first year, explaining when to introduce solids, how to prepare foods and eventually how to encourage a healthy eating pattern during toddlerhood.

It may be that you are not strictly vegetarian, or do not intend to bring up your baby with a meat-free diet, but I hope there are many suggestions and plenty of information included in this book that will help you have a healthy pregnancy and your baby have the best start in life.

About Health Before and During Pregnancy

It is widely known that a mother's diet and her health during pregnancy are important both to the mother herself and to the growing baby. Now we are becoming increasingly aware that her condition in the months leading up to pregnancy also matters.

If you are thinking about becoming pregnant and are in a situation where you are able to plan, then it makes sense to review your diet and lifestyle. Give yourself a chance to get in good condition. The main reason is that you will be in better shape to cope with the changes the pregnancy brings. Of course, you don't have to be a superwoman to cope with pregnancy, but the fitter you are the more chance you have of having a happy, healthy time and a happy, healthy baby. Both the pregnancy and the early months with the baby are very demanding and it is useful to have resources on which to draw. Secondary reasons for getting in good shape now are that it can't do the child any harm, it may make conception easier, and you'll feel good for it.

Research on whether you have a better chance of conceiving if you are healthy is still in its early stages. Evidence so far indicates that it is likely, and it is also thought that your chances of conceiving will be higher if you are not overweight. Note, though, that conception takes two! So it is a good idea if you can involve your partner in your healthier regime. Then you can both feel the benefit. This will also act as a little morale booster, especially on 'cutting down/out' activity – such as alcohol or smoking.

Another point about having a good diet while you are trying to get pregnant is that you can't be sure when you will actually conceive. It may be the first time you try; it may be several months later. Ninety per cent of women are pregnant within twelve months of trying. If you plan to leave considerations of diet until you know you are pregnant, then that may be quite difficult. You may feel unable to take certain foods then. Also, bear in mind that there may well be a time when you are not sure if you are pregnant or not – so that's another reason for starting to eat well as soon as possible.

I would recommend at least three months of taking care of yourself before you conceive. If by chance you become pregnant more quickly than you expect, don't panic. Just check through your diet and start straight away making changes for the better.

Apart from your diet there are a number of other things you should consider once you plan to become pregnant and during your pregnancy.

Immunity to Rubella (German Measles)

It always struck me as odd that the notices to tell you to check you were immune to rubella were prominently displayed in the antenatal clinic. By then it is too late, as you cannot be immunised once you are pregnant. To find out whether you are immune, ask your doctor to take a blood test. If you are not immune you will need an injection and it is important not to become pregnant for one month afterwards.

Rubella can be very damaging or even fatal to your baby, especially if you contract the disease in the first fourteen weeks of pregnancy, so even though an infection is an extremely unlikely chance it is worth seeing your doctor and taking some action.

Coming off the Pill

It is advisable to stop taking the pill some time before you try to conceive. The pill alters the make-up of your blood and it needs three months or so for it to return to normal (although if you did conceive during this time there would be no harm to the foetus). Having a gap also allows your monthly cycle a chance to return to normal. About a third of all women find this happens within a month. About one in fifty may have to wait six months. If you are having regular periods it makes it easier to work out when your baby is due.

Smoking

Smoking during pregnancy has been shown to be harmful to the baby in several ways. Smokers, especially those on more than twenty cigarettes a day, have a slightly greater chance of aborting. There is a higher risk of the baby being premature and the baby's birth weight is likely to be 150–300 g (5–11 oz) less than average. As carbon monoxide passes from your cigarette via your lungs into your bloodstream, your baby receives less oxygen and cannot grow as well as it should. Babies of low birth weight are more prone to infection or other complications after the birth.

If you think you will find it difficult to give up in pregnancy, try to stop smoking before. There is all sorts of specialist advice available. Perhaps the health of your baby may be the inspiration for you to break the habit.

Alcohol

Alcohol has also been shown to affect fertility (both for men and women). You may increase your chance of conceiving if you don't drink.

Heavy drinking is certainly not advisable during pregnancy as the alcohol which enters your bloodstream passes across the placenta into the baby's blood. Once again, the earliest weeks of the baby's development are the most critical. Unfortunately this is a time when many women do not realise they are pregnant, which is why it is worth cutting down or giving up alcohol as soon as you plan to have a baby. Although evidence shows that sustained drinking or even a heavy binge can be harmful to the developing foetus by causing growth retardation, developmental delay and neurological abnormalities, it is not known what is a safe limit. If you are able to give up, then probably no drinking is best. If you can't manage this, limit yourself to two or three units a week. A unit is a glass of wine, half a pint of beer or a single measure of spirits (including sherry). Socially it is easier than ever before not to drink alcohol as soft drinks are generally on offer at most functions. You are likely for a number of reasons to be thirstier during pregnancy; look at the section on drinks to give you some ideas on tipples that might help you forget alcohol.

Caffeine

Drinking coffee isn't going to be a serious health hazard to you and your baby. However caffeine can upset your digestive system and block the absorption of some nutrients. It can also make it harder for you to relax and can cause sleeplessness (though maybe all mothers-to-be should get used to this?). Many women find they go off these drinks anyway. I did initially. Even the thought of the coffee pot made me feel ill. There are lots of caffeine-free alternatives such as grain coffee, carob drinks, and an enormous variety of herbal teas amongst which you'll probably find something you like. See the section on what to drink for more ideas.

Drugs and Medicines

You shouldn't take any drugs or medicines, especially in the early part of pregnancy. If you do need medication, you should check with your doctor as some drugs can be fine in early pregnancy but not later. This advice doesn't just apply to prescriptions as there are many things that can be bought over the counter (for headaches or indigestion etc.) that can harm the foetus. Obviously if you have a medical condition that requires regular medicine you should discuss this with your doctor if there is any likelihood of your becoming pregnant. If you are taking homoeopathic remedies, you should check these with your homoeopath.

Exercise

Pregnancy isn't like scaling Everest or running a marathon, though it can seem like that sometimes. You will cope better with the tiredness and inevitable weight gain if you are reasonably fit to start with. Your level of fitness is relevant to you. If you already do a fair amount of exercise such as swimming, running, cycling etc., there is no reason why you should stop, certainly for the first half to two-thirds of your pregnancy. You must, of course, listen to your body and stop or do less if you feel any discomfort. If you have never taken any exercise, it is not the time to rush madly into daily aerobic sessions, but you could try to take up something gentle such as swimming a couple of times a week or having a brisk daily walk. There are also suggestions in the exercise chapter for routines you can do at home to give you a general tone up. These are best done in conjunction with some sort of light physical activity.

Pregnancy and Nutrition

Pregnancy is a great motivator; think, for example, of all the 'nest-feathering' that people tend to do, getting rooms ready for a larger family! The same is true of your own well-being – you'll probably start to think carefully about it. It may well be a time when you are more concerned with and more aware of your body than at any other period of your life. Trips to the doctors, jumping on and off scales, blood tests and blood pressure, the hormonal changes, all make you focus on your general state of health. Often, especially with a first pregnancy, there is very little showing externally for the first four to five months. I was still wearing my normal clothes, including running kit, until four and a half months, though one or two of my sharper-eyed friends thought my waistline had expanded a little. Even though there is little to see on the surface, there is a tremendous amount going on inside. It is a critical growth period for the baby. The nervous system begins to develop in the third week, and by the eleventh week all the major organs such as the heart, brain, kidneys and liver are formed, though not mature.

As the growing baby depends on you entirely for his first nine months' nutrition, it seems common sense that the better quality you can offer, the better start he will have.

You may have had time to review your diet already. If not, do it now. One factor that may influence whether or not you have a healthy diet is if you don't feel like eating. In the first three months or so of your pregnancy you may well suffer from morning sickness – a slight misnomer in that it can go on all day! Read the advice on page 48 to see ways that you can cope with it. Once again it will help if you are well nourished before pregnancy so your body has resources to draw on should the need occur.

What Do You Need from Your Diet?

I felt it was a good idea to have a quick refresher course on how to eat healthily, whether you are pregnant or not. It is much easier to sustain healthy eating if you know the what and why of nutritious foods. Let's look both at what nutrients you need and the role they play in your body, as well as the increased requirements for some nutrients during pregnancy.

Whatever your diet, whether it contains no meat or fish, no dairy produce or eggs, or a little of all these things, the food you eat breaks down into the five essential nutrients:

- proteins
- carbohydrates
- fats
- vitamins
- minerals

The sources of these nutrients vary depending on your diet. There is no reason to suggest that a diet free of meat and fish will leave you short of any nutrient during pregnancy.

Protein

Protein promotes growth and forms the framework of different body structures such as skin and hair. As well as enabling growth, proteins are also used to repair and maintain these structures. Proteins are needed to maintain supplies of enzymes, hormones and antibodies which help regulate body functions.

Proteins are made up of a number of amino acids. Eight of these are known as the essential amino acids as, unlike the others, the body cannot synthesise them. Since the body cannot make them they need to be somewhere in the diet. Fortunately these essential amino acids are found in different proportions in numerous foods. No single vegetable food contains an ideal mixture of these amino acids, so in a vegetarian diet it is important to eat a variety of foods that contain proteins to give the body an ideal supply. The main vegetarian food groups that supply protein are:

- pulses (beans, peas and lentils)
- nuts and seeds
- grains
- dairy produce

These groups each contain different amounts of the essential amino acids. The body is happy to find its requirements from a mix of foods. When two of the above groups are combined together, ideally in the same meal, the amino acid profiles are complementary and the body ends up with a good supply. Foods from these different groups should be eaten every day.

When you are not pregnant, as long as you are eating a wide variety of the vegetarian staples (cereals, pulses, nuts and seeds), it is unlikely that you will be short of protein. During your pregnancy your need for protein will increase as your growing baby will need his share too. Again, as long as you are eating a good variety of the sources of protein you are unlikely to be short, but it is wise to make a bit more effort if you have been tending to snack or rush or skip meals.

Good Sources of Protein
All foods in the groups mentioned – pulses (beans, peas, and lentils), grains (including cereals and flours), nuts and seeds, and dairy produce – will provide you with some protein. Just to give you some idea, the foods listed below yield some of the highest amounts. However, if one of your favourites isn't mentioned, carry on eating it. See the meal ideas with suggestions on how the foods can be combined into good protein meals.

- From the grain family, protein is found in:
  whole wheat, wholewheat flour and by-products such as pasta; oatmeal and oatflakes

- From the pulse family:
  chick peas, lentils, split peas, tofu and haricot beans

- From nuts and seeds, protein is found in:
  peanuts, almonds, walnuts and Brazil nuts

- From dairy produce:
  Cheddar cheese, cottage cheese, egg yolks and yoghurt

It isn't difficult to combine the different food groups to make meals that contain a good supply of protein. I always found when creating recipes that it happened almost naturally. If you make a bean casserole, for example, it is best served with rice, pasta or potato as these drier ingredients work well with the more liquid stew. This combination of beans and grains achieves the complementary protein mix desired. If you make a nut roast or burger, you'll need to add something like breadcrumbs, oatflakes or flour to bulk up and thicken the mixture. Once again, this combination of nuts and grains yields an excellent amount and blend of protein. Apart from the ideas in the recipe section, there are many other examples of protein foods working well together, such as beans on toast, hummus and pitta bread, almond paella or lentil lasagne. Don't forget that you can also make combinations in sweet dishes such as a nut and oat crumble topping, or a mixed muesli with grains, nuts and seeds.

Carbohydrates

Carbohydrates give us energy, help the body to use protein and play an important role in maintaining the central nervous system. There are two main types of carbohydrate: sugars or simple carbohydrates, and starches or complex carbohydrates. Sucrose is the common sugar that is used to sweeten cakes, biscuits and so on. Sucrose does provide energy (calories) but unfortunately nothing else in the way of nutrients. The starches are far better in that regard. They include foods such as whole grains (wheat, rice, for example) and potatoes. They are absorbed more slowly into the body giving more sustained levels of energy rather than sudden boosts and drops. Complex carbohydrates, as well as providing calories, also tend to include proteins, useful vitamins, minerals and fibre.

During pregnancy – and afterwards – you will need plenty of energy. You'll probably eat more and therefore take in extra calories. Try to fill yourself up with naturally satisfying, bulky foods such as bread, cereals and potatoes. These will keep you going but shouldn't mean you put on unnecessary weight. You will obviously weigh more as the pregnancy develops but you should aim to control your weight and not just get fat. This will place added strain on the body during your pregnancy, and it will be depressing when you have to do something about it afterwards.

Good Sources of Carbohydrate
All unrefined grains such as brown rice, bulgar wheat, buckwheat, wholemeal pasta are carbohydrate-rich. These are also useful sources of the vitamin B group. You can also get carbohydrates from potatoes which are also a source of vitamin C, as well as beans, peas and lentils.

Fats

Fat is a highly concentrated form of energy. In other words, a little fat contains a lot of calories. Eating a lot of fatty foods means you are liable to become fat. Should you try and avoid fat altogether? Certainly not. Fat has several important functions. It helps keep the body warm by being stored in layers under the skin. Fatty tissues store fat soluble vitamins A, D, E and K which are all essential for life. During pregnancy extra fat is stored for the body to draw on later when extra resources are needed during breast feeding. Women who breast feed may find they lose weight easily during the breast feeding months. The key thing to bear in mind is the eating of the right type of fat and doing so only in moderation.

There are three main types of fat: saturated, monosaturated and polyunsaturated. No single food contains only one sort of fat and a constant debate rages as to whether one type of fat is better than another. Saturated fats are generally considered unhealthy. These fats (which are often from animal sources, such as meat fat and dairy produce) are thought to increase levels of cholesterol in the blood. Polyunsaturated fats eaten in small quantities are thought to be healthy. They contain essential fatty acids that the body cannot function well without, and they do not increase levels of cholesterol. Some research has indicated that these fats may even help these levels decrease slightly. Apart from coconut and palm oil, most fats found in the vegetable kingdom tend to be polyunsaturated or monosaturated (which have no effect on cholesterol levels).

Both pre-pregnancy and during pregnancy your fat intake should be less than one-third of your overall diet. There is no need for fat levels to be increased during pregnancy. Your body will convert carbohydrate into any extra fat stores that are needed. If you are the sort of vegetarian who relies quite heavily on eggs and cheese, try to get into the habit of using some of the other staples, such as pulses, nuts and cereals, to make your meals. Look at the suggestions in the text on proteins and carbohydrates.

Good Sources of Fats

Oils
Sunflower oil is an excellent all-round ingredient for cooking and for salad dressings. It is worth looking for varieties known as cold pressed (usually on sale in health food shops) because they have undergone less processing and thus retain more nutrients and also more flavour.

Olive oil is a monosaturated or neutral fat. It is a versatile oil that can be used for both cooking and salad dressings.

Avoid coconut and palm oils as they are saturated. Beware of unspecified vegetable oils as these are often made with these ingredients.

Nuts and Seeds

Apart from their fat content, nuts and seeds give you a range of vitamins and minerals, depending on the variety of nut or seed, so it is useful to incorporate them in your diet. Most nuts work well in sweet or savoury dishes. They also make good snacks, but remember that a little should go a long way. If you have a craving for salted nuts while you are pregnant, a healthier way to combat this craving is to roast your own nuts and seeds in a little shoyu or soy sauce. In this way you get a salty flavour without so much salt and without the extra oil in which the nuts are generally roasted.

Dairy Products

During pregnancy you may well be advised to eat more dairy products because of the importance of getting enough calcium (see page 17). Remember, though, that the fats in dairy products (milk as well as cheese) are mainly saturated. Low fat varieties and skimmed or semi-skimmed milk are worth considering as these products are no lower in calcium than the full fat varieties. You may notice no difference in taste.

Vitamins

Although vitamins are only required by the body in minute quantities, they are vital to our well-being. They act in numerous capacities such as fighting infection, keeping skin healthy, proper functioning of the brain and circulatory systems, and preventing haemorrhaging. There are two groups of vitamins: water soluble (the vitamin B group, vitamin C and folic acid) and fat soluble (vitamins A, D, E, K). Vitamins tend to be fragile and depending on the type are easily destroyed by cooking, heat, light or exposure to air. The water soluble vitamins cannot be stored for long in the body so constant supplies are needed. Fat soluble vitamins are stored for longer in fatty tissues. Chemicals in substances such as alcohol, cigarettes and coffee use up extra vitamin resources. You'll do yourself a favour by reducing intake of these things whether you are pregnant or not! While you are pregnant you need extra resources of all vitamins, particularly vitamin C, folic acid, B_{12} and vitamin D.

Vitamin C

You may remember from your school history lessons how a disease called scurvy was a hazard of long sea journeys in olden days. This was caused by a limited supply of fresh produce and a consequent shortage of vitamin C.

Vitamin C has many uses in the body. During pregnancy your need for vitamin C will increase, as this is the vitamin that helps absorption of iron. Vegetarians don't have any worries about supplies of this vitamin as fruit and vegetables are a rich source. Particularly good are the citrus family, including oranges, grapefruit and lemons; soft summer fruits such as strawberries, raspberries and blackcurrants; and green vegetables such as sprouts, broccoli, cabbage, spinach and leeks. Bean sprouts are also an excellent source and can be eaten in salads or thrown at the very last minute into the stir-fried dishes.

Vitamin C is a water soluble vitamin and is rather fragile, being sensitive to heat and light. Produce containing vitamin C should be eaten as fresh as possible. Store items such as fruit and vegetables in a cool dark place and try to eat some raw fruit and vegetables daily.

Folic Acid

This vitamin is a member of the B group. It is vital for the healthy development of the baby's central nervous system as well as major organs and tissues. A recent large scale study of pregnant women has produced evidence that a sufficiency of folic acid may prevent some severe birth defects such as spina bifida and hydrocephalus. Folic acid deficiency can also contribute to anaemia which is something to watch for in the mother-to-be. The recommendations are that all pregnant women and those planning to become pregnant should be offered folic acid tablets as a supplement. There is no evidence to show that the vitamin is toxic. (More on this under iron page 18.) You may consider taking a supplement. There are many foods on a vegetarian diet that contain folic acid. It occurs in pulses, green vegetables, oranges, wholewheat products such as bread, pasta and pastry. It is also found in yeast extracts which are ideal for savoury snacks.

Like vitamin C, folic acid is sensitive to heat. Store vegetables in cool dark places out of their polythene wrappings. Try to eat some dark green vegetables raw, or at least only lightly steamed.

Vitamin B_{12}

This is essential for the function of most body cells. It also helps in the synthesis of DNA which is present in the nucleus of every cell to enable it to divide. B_{12} is present in ample quantities in dairy products such as cottage cheese or milk. Anyone who is vegan or not able to eat dairy foods for some reason should take particular care to have a sufficient supply of vitamin B_{12}. One of the best non-dairy sources of this vitamin is a fortified soya milk which may contain twice as much B_{12} as ordinary cows' milk. There are a couple of fortified brands on the market which may be available in your supermarket or health food shop. Soya milk can be used to make white sauces, put on cereal and added to drinks. It doesn't taste like cows' milk, but if you think about it as a different product it is quite acceptable. Margarines fortified with B_{12} are also available from health food shops. A third useful source is yeast extract. Vitamin supplements, from non-animal sources, are also available.

Vitamin D
This vitamin helps absorption of calcium. It is present in fortified margarines but the best (and cheapest) source is sunshine. Don't immediately book a foreign holiday if you are having a winter baby! The body stores vitamin D efficiently. Simply getting out for an hour or so on sunny days should do the trick.

Minerals
Minerals are part of the structural framework of the body and are present in bones, teeth and muscle fibres. Like vitamins, they have numerous vital roles in the body. Minerals help the body break down and utilise food. They also help the muscles contract and relax.

Although each mineral has a different function, they often work together in groups. For example calcium, which is an essential part of an antenatal diet, is a major component of bones and teeth. It teams up with phosphorus to maintain healthy bones, while magnesium helps the body use the calcium that is present. The presence of copper helps iron work more efficiently. Sodium and potassium are also interdependent and both are needed for biological functions such as maintaining the body water balance and the acid-base balance as well as transmission of electrical impulses along nerve fibres and into muscles.

Calcium
Calcium is needed by the growing foetus for bones and teeth. Whilst the baby is growing in the womb his first teeth begin to form in his gums after about three months. (Very occasionally a baby is born with a tooth already showing.)

Easily available sources are dairy products such as milk,

cheese, butter and yoghurt. Bear in mind the advice about too much fat in your diet and go for the skimmed and low fat varieties. These are just as high in calcium.

If you are vegan or don't eat dairy foods, there are other sources of calcium. Soya products such as tofu, soya milk and soya flour are all excellent sources. Tofu can be used to make main courses, either sweet or savoury. It works particularly well in dishes with a sauce as it will then absorb the flavours of the other ingredients. Otherwise, try it marinaded in something like a vinaigrette and baked. For sweet dishes use tofu as you would yoghurt. Mix it with fruit purées to make fools and whips. Soya flour can be added to any ordinary dough (pastry or bread) or cake and biscuit mixtures. Small quantities such as a tablespoon won't change the flavour; if anything it makes the mixture a little richer.

Broccoli, okra and kale contain useful amounts of calcium as does blackstrap molasses – a potential sweetening ingredient of bread, puddings and biscuits.

Almonds, Brazil nuts and sesame seeds are also good sources. Have these as nibbles, or use them in sweet or savoury dishes. There is plenty of calcium in tahini, the paste made from sesame seeds. Use it as a savoury spread thinned with water, or as a base for a salad dressing. Mixed with yoghurt or curd cheese it makes a delicious creamy dip. It also works well when mixed with lentil or chick pea purées to make a savoury pâté.

Iron
Iron is needed to make haemoglobin, the oxygen-carrying component of blood. Shortage of iron leads to anaemia, which is a shortage of red blood corpuscles. It is a common condition. Your need for iron increases during pregnancy, both to cope with the extra volume of blood you build up in your own body as well as the iron supplied to your growing baby. He takes enough from you to last for his first six months in the world.

In the average meat-eater's diet, the source of 25 per cent of iron is meat. So if you don't eat meat, there is in theory the chance that you could only be eating three-quarters of the iron you need. If you are careful, however, there should be no reason, as a vegetarian or vegan, for you to be short of iron. Do make sure you know which foods contain iron. Be prepared to convince doctors that not all vegetarians are anaemic. I had to! The moment I mentioned being vegetarian (although my haemoglobin count was normal), the word was written on the top of my notes and then highlighted. I was immediately interrogated as to where I thought I was getting my iron from and almost prescribed a rump steak.

You will be given a blood test on your first antenatal visit which will show whether or not you are anaemic. As the body is able to store iron it is worth starting to build up a reserve before pregnancy. Do this by eating iron-rich foods. You need to eat plenty of these as iron is poorly absorbed. Continue this practice throughout pregnancy.

Good sources of iron are dried fruits such as peaches, apricots, figs, raisins and prunes. A 100 g (4 oz) serving of millet would contain nearly half a day's supply. Wheatgerm is also a good source. Put some in your morning cereal, add it to cake, pastry and bread mixtures as well as savoury dishes such as nut or lentil bakes. Remember because of its fat content wheatgerm doesn't have that long a shelf life. Buy small quantities, store it in a cool place and aim to use up a packet quickly. Haricot beans and lentils will provide you with some iron, so will bread, flour, oatmeal and other cereals. Green vegetables such as broccoli, kale and parsley are also good sources. It is true that spinach contains more iron than other leafy vegetables. However, the iron from it is poorly absorbed. It also contains high proportions of oxalic acid which reduces the availability of calcium from food eaten at the same time.

Remember your absorption of iron will increase if you eat it along with foods rich in vitamin C.

If you do become short of iron, there are tablets which can be prescribed. Be aware that these can have unappealing side effects such as constipation, nausea or giddiness. If you take tablets and find they don't suit you, ask to swap to another type. I had one blood test towards the end of my pregnancy which showed my haemoglobin level was very slightly under par. After two days of tablets that had some of the side effects mentioned, I abandoned them and boosted myself with lots of iron-rich food which brought the levels up in a much more pleasant fashion.

Putting It All Together: A Healthy Diet for you and the Growing Baby

Once you know what you need to eat and why, the next stage is trying to put it all together. It can seem daunting to work out exactly what is a healthy diet. Are you eating the right balance of amino acids? Which vitamin helps iron absorption? You may well have other things to think about!

Nutrition is a relatively new and fascinating subject. The good news is that, whilst there has been much confusion about exactly what is a healthy diet, there are some simple guidelines which are easy to follow, particularly if you are vegetarian.

It may be that overall your diet is quite good. However, bearing in mind your changed state, it is worth checking and making alterations where necessary. Follow these guidelines while you are preparing for pregnancy as well as during pregnancy. When you do become pregnant, be sure to include foods that are rich in vital nutrients, such as iron and calcium, in your diet.

Get Fresh
You'll get the best from your foods if they are fresh, particularly fruit and vegetables. Try to shop frequently for these items. In general they need to be kept in cool places, out of the light. Take them out of any polythene or shrink wrappings. Many vegetarian staples such as grains and pulses have long shelf lives and don't deteriorate nutritionally. Exceptions are nuts and seeds which you shouldn't store too long. Their high fat content means they can go rancid. It's also best to keep grains in a cool cupboard. Wheatgerm should be kept in the refrigerator.

A Balancing Act
The key words for any healthy diet are balance and variety. Don't eat an excess of anything but eat plenty of different things. You may get cravings which you can't do much about. Once they pass try to get back to a more wide-ranging eating pattern.

Fillers not Fatteners
Make sure your diet contains plenty of unrefined carbohydrates and fibre. This includes foods such as potatoes and grains in all forms – flours, flakes and pastas. These foods will fill you up, give you energy and provide you with a good supply of fibre which should prevent you getting constipated – a common problem in pregnancy.

The myth that starches are fattening still persists. It is not the starches that are fattening but the things we tend to put with them such as a big dollop of butter with a baked potato or a rich cream sauce with pasta.

More than an Apple a Day
Try to eat at least four or five helpings of fresh fruit and vegetables per day or more if you like. Go for as much variety as possible to

maximise the range of vitamins. It is fairly unlikely that you will overdo it. There are the usual old wives' tales about too many strawberries causing strawberry birthmarks, but there is no evidence to back this up. Most fruit and vegetables are rich sources of many vitamins and minerals. The fresher they are the more of these nutrients you get, so it does pay to shop for them frequently. Also, try to keep both fruit and vegetables in a cool, dark place to preserve the vitamins, unless it is something like an avocado pear or some tropical fruit that needs to ripen.

Remember that the less you cook a fruit or vegetable the more nutrients you will preserve in it. Make sure you have at least one good bowlful of salad a day, or chunks of raw vegetable with a dip made from yoghurt or tahini. If you prefer cooked vegetables, steaming, stir-frying and microwaving are all ways of cooking that preserve the maximum vitamins.

The natural sweetness of fruit should help you if you get a craving for sweet things during pregnancy. Eat fruit as a snack between meals. Try to use it as a basis for puddings. I've given some ideas, along these lines, in the recipe section (see page 139). Add fruit to salads: oranges, apples and peaches work particularly well.

Dried fruits are also a useful source of nutrients. These can be eaten without soaking as a sweet treat, but do remember they are highly concentrated foods with a high calorie content. So eat them sparingly.

Another reason for eating vegetables and fruit is that they are a good source of dietary fibre.

A Bit Thin on Fats

Switch to polyunsaturated fats and try to eat less fat overall. Luckily for vegetarians most saturated fats are found in meat. Look at the paragraph on fats (see page 14) for information on sources of polyunsaturated and monosaturated fats and suggestions on how to incorporate them into your diet. It is not difficult to adjust the amount of fat you add to your own food. You can switch to skimmed milk products and have less fried foods for example. What you have to watch out for is processed or ready made foods that have a hidden fat content. Items such as cakes, biscuits and pastries all contain high levels of fats. Snack foods such as crisps, corn chips, roasted nuts and ice-cream are also culprits. In pregnancy you may well get a craving for these foods. Try to divert your craving to something better. If this is impossible, try to balance your diet to take account of your craving. If you have just wolfed down a jumbo bag of crisps, use a low fat cheese in your sandwiches.

Naturally Sweet

Try to eat less sugar, whatever the type. Whilst you do need extra energy and calories to cope with pregnancy, getting these calories simply from sugar such as that in sweets will not enrich your diet. Sugar provides you with nothing but calories. In metabolising sugar, useful stores of vitamins and minerals are depleted. It is easy to consume extra calories with these foods which will be stored by the body as fat. Some of these bulges will not shift easily once you get rid of the main bulge after nine months. The other thing to consider is your teeth, which are more vulnerable in pregnancy. As usual the old wives have something to say on the subject. This time the story goes that you lose a tooth for every baby. The baby is supposed to pinch all your calcium, leaving your teeth weakened. The truth is that, due to hormonal changes, your gums may become swollen and sore. These conditions are not helped if you eat too many sweet things. Fortunately, in Britain, you have the right to free dental treatment during your pregnancy and for the first year of your baby's life. As with fat 'naughties' you may well get a craving for sweet things that you wouldn't normally dream of eating if you weren't pregnant. Try to switch to less damaging nibbles such as scones and fruit buns rather than cakes and pastries. Again, find sweet alternatives such as fruit.

See Salt Less

Once people are on a wholefood diet, their need for lots of salt seems to diminish. If you still eat a lot of salt, start cutting down now. A high salt diet has been linked to high blood pressure. This condition won't change overnight but you can do something to improve it. It is best to have a normal to low blood pressure when you become pregnant. There might be some change in your blood pressure during pregnancy anyway. Blood pressure is an indicator of how efficiently your heart is pumping the blood around the body. In pregnancy, your heart also pumps blood into the placenta which is how your baby receives food and oxygen. High blood pressure can mean that you may be pumping less blood into the placenta than is necessary. With some women, high blood pressure can also be an indication of a condition known as pre-eclampsia (see page 50). If you do get high blood pressure, you will be very closely monitored and the problems can usually be dealt with.

Apart from adding salt to foods — something which you can easily stop — be aware that highly processed foods can contain large quantities of salt, as well as fat and sugar. Snack foods such as salted nuts and crisps are obvious examples.

Whilst I very rarely use salt, I am a great fan of shoyu (soy sauce). It does contain some salt so if you use a vast amount, cut down a little.

Food Scares

In the last few years concern about the safety of some foods has increased. The food production chain from source to your table is long and complicated. There is ample opportunity for contamination to occur. In many instances, these scares only concern vulnerable groups which, as a healthy woman, probably hasn't had to concern you. Once you are pregnant, despite your good health it can come as a shock to realise you are one of those at risk.

The main infections that pregnant women should be aware of are poisoning from the bacteria salmonella and listeria as well as toxoplasmosis.

Salmonella

Salmonella can make you very ill but the unborn child is very very rarely infected as salmonella is confined to the digestive tract. It does not normally enter the blood stream and cross the placenta. The reason why you should take precautions to avoid salmonella poisoning when you are pregnant is that it can have a dehydrating effect which may cause problems.

Salmonella is found mostly in meat products which have been badly cooked or stored, but it can also be found in eggs – free range as well as battery produced. If an egg is thoroughly boiled, in other words hard boiled, then it is safe, as any bacteria will have been destroyed. It is also fine to use eggs in cake mixtures or baking and for savoury dishes such as roasts and burgers. Lightly cooked eggs such as poached, soft-boiled or sloppy omelettes are risky. So too is home-made mayonnaise as the eggs are used raw. Shop-bought mayonnaise is thought to be safe as the eggs are pasteurised. It is easy to avoid the egg dishes mentioned for the short time you are pregnant. If you are keen on mayonnaise as a salad dressing there are plenty of alternatives. For creamy mixtures use yoghurt, sour cream or soft tofu combined with oils, garlic, lemon juice, herbs, or nut or seed butters or ground nuts. There are plenty of tips in the recipe section.

Listeria

This infection can affect the baby in pregnancy and may cause a miscarriage and still birth. In some cases the pregnant woman is not seriously ill, perhaps experiencing a mild flu, but the baby may still be damaged. As the extent of damage to the baby is difficult to predict, the Department of Health recommends that all pregnant women and those planning to be pregnant avoid certain foods and ready-made meals particularly the cook-chill variety and shop-bought salads, both ready-prepared dressed salads and chopped pre-prepared salad ingredients.

Listeria can also be found in soil which is why it is important to scrub or peel vegetables and it can also thrive in low temperatures. Avoid ready-made salads (one of the worst offenders are bean sprout salads). Make your own. This will be safer as you can be sure the salad ingredients are thoroughly washed and stored in a cold refrigerator. If you take salad ingredients as part of a lunch time snack at work, take items such as well washed tomatoes, sticks of celery and whole radishes as these shouldn't cause a problem.

If you buy a cook-chill meal such as a quiche or pizza, it must be heated thoroughly before eating. Use a conventional oven rather than a microwave which may leave cool spots in the food. Listeria can re-colonise after pasteurisation. You should avoid soft ripe cheese such as Brie and Camembert as well as blue veined cheese such as Danish Blue or Stilton. Goat and sheep products can also be affected.

Toxoplasmosis
Toxoplasmosis is an infection caused by the parasite *Toxoplasma gondii*. It is only dangerous to humans if their immune system is undeveloped, as in an unborn child. Cats and undercooked meat are thought to be the principle sources of human infection. Cat faeces may remain infected for up to 14 months and can therefore contaminate the soil. Vegetables which have been exposed to the parasite can also be a source of infection. Babies that are infected early on in pregnancy may be miscarried or stillborn. Babies that are born with Toxoplasmosis may develop severe symptoms resulting in mental retardation, epilepsy and blindness. You may be immune to Toxoplasmosis. If you want to find out, ask for a simple blood test at your antenatal clinic or ask your doctor. Ideally you should do this before you become pregnant. If you are not immune, you should take the following precautions. Get someone else to empty the cat litter tray. Always wear gloves for gardening and wash your hands after touching soil. Always wash fruit and vegetables thoroughly. Avoid unpasteurised milk products and unpasteurised milk. Cover children's outdoor sand boxes.

Weight gain

You will gain weight during your pregnancy. It is not just the growing baby that causes this but an increase in bodily fluids. This includes extra blood, the development of the placenta, enlargement of the uterus, fat stored for breast feeding and enlarged breasts. How much should this all come to? It can vary from one woman to another but a weight gain of 20–28 lb during the nine months is typical. This weight should be gained at roughly 1 lb a month during the first three months, then about 3 lb a month for the second trimester, and finally at 1 lb a week during the last phase. If you keep a check you will notice if you have a sudden weight gain. A steady increase in weight through your pregnancy is best as it gives you more time to adjust.

It is important not to get overweight during pregnancy. It will put a strain on your muscles and ligaments, increase your fatigue and add to the risk of varicose veins. Too much extra fat makes it hard to measure and assess the foetus. It can also be depressing to be overweight once your baby is born. You shouldn't diet during pregnancy. If you start to miss out on nutrients your baby will miss out too. It is true to say that you are eating for two. Just remember that one of those two is pretty tiny. What is vital is that you take in a plentiful supply of good quality food.

If you are already overweight (or underweight) and thinking about having a baby, it is worth trying to do something about that before getting pregnant. Adopt a healthy eating regime and perhaps even more importantly, find a type of exercise you enjoy doing. Obviously, if during your pregnancy you are putting on an excessive amount of weight through over eating and bingeing on some of the baddies already mentioned, then you should cut those out of your diet. Switch to worthwhile sources of calories such as sandwiches and cereals. Skip the cakes and ice-cream!

The Early Months

Your pregnancy starts officially from the first day of the last period you had before you conceived. This is usually about two weeks before conception took place. To work out when the baby is due, calculate forty weeks from that official start day.

Forty weeks has been used for some time as the average figure for all women for all pregnancies. It is used as a reference scale for study and writing on pregnancy. It works well. Nevertheless when it comes to your pregnancy you will be the exception if your pregnancy is exactly that long. I read that a recent study had found that women like me – white women expecting their first child – have pregnancies that average longer than the forty weeks.

For purposes of study, pregnancy is divided into three equal time periods referred to as trimesters. Each trimester has different characteristics. It is useful to understand something of what happens in each trimester, both to you and to the baby growing inside you.

First of all, how do you even know if you are pregnant? Missing a period is generally the first thing women notice, especially if they are used to having a regular monthly cycle. You may also experience tingling or slightly swollen breasts. Other signs include a need to nip to the loo more often, being constipated, more vaginal discharge than usual, or a feeling of nausea.

You can do DIY pregnancy tests, bought from a chemist, from as early as two days after your period is due. These tests claim to be 99 per cent accurate in laboratory conditions. If you have any doubt about the reading you get, it is best to do the test again three or more days later. You can also go to the doctor for a free test but it can take longer to get the results. Even if the result is positive, doctors may be inclined to do little at this stage as miscarriage in these first few weeks is very common; as many as one in three pregnancies may end in this way. However it is very difficult to document the extent of these early miscarriages as they may appear to be no more than a late and slightly heavier period. With confirmed pregnancies one in six are lost before the end of the first trimester.

Once you have missed two periods and are therefore roughly eight weeks pregnant then go back to the doctor. That is the time to discuss where the baby might be born (at home, hospital etc.). If you are going to hospital, the doctor will give you a letter so you can arrange your first antenatal appointment.

What is Happening to You

The first trimester is the part of your pregnancy up to about fourteen weeks and is a time of enormous hormonal changes. There will be few outward physical signs to show you are pregnant. It may take you until about week five or six even to realise you might be pregnant, and with some women much longer.

Your breasts may increase a little in size but it is unlikely your waistline or tummy will expand much at all. You may have some physical discomforts, particularly nausea or 'morning sickness', which affects about half of all pregnant women during the early weeks. There are some things you can try to overcome this (see page 48). You may also feel extremely tired during this stage. This is due to the massive hormonal changes taking place in your body which will enable you to support your growing baby.

This first trimester can also be a rather emotional time. The sickness and tiredness may make you feel rather depressed. Be comforted that these feelings should pass. You are probably also adjusting to the fact that you are pregnant and some of the implications that will have. Talking out your worries can help, but it may be that you want to keep your pregnancy secret just now.

My own pregnancy followed a fairly classic pattern. The first thing I noticed apart from missing a period, was a different feeling in my breasts and a change in size. From the sixth week, I had bouts of morning sickness. I was usually fine first thing but about half way through the morning I would get a horrid taste in my mouth. Sometimes I felt a little short of breath and rather panicky. I remember if I happened to be out of the house and this feeling came over me, I would talk to myself. Anything to encourage me to get home. This caused some very quizzical looks. I felt I needed a T-shirt that said 'Don't think I'm crazy, just pregnant'. In the early months, I also went off coffee. I couldn't even bear to think of it in the cup. Luckily I enjoy herbal teas and found plenty of interesting blends and flavours to substitute.

What I found particularly frustrating was the awful tiredness in those early weeks. I couldn't believe I could be so exhausted with nothing to show, no extra weight to carry and plenty of sleep at night. Some days found me struggling to get out of bed. Luckily working from home meant my journey to the office was simply a matter of walking into the next room. I didn't have to worry about anyone moaning at me if I only staggered in at midday.

What is Happening Inside

Whilst not much is going on on the surface, there is frantic activity inside! The first fourteen weeks are of immense importance to the baby. After conception in week two, the fertilised egg travels into the womb where it settles into the lining. At this point two different types of cell start to develop. Some will become the placenta which separates the mother's and baby's circulation and provides nourishment for the baby in the womb. Other cells will form the organs of the embryo. From about week three or four, the neural tube starts to form; this will eventually become the brain and spinal cord. The heart starts to develop and starts beating by around week six. Blood vessels develop to form the umbilical cord. This links the baby with the mother's placenta. Blood with vital oxygen and food is transported through the cord, and waste matter carried away. Other major organs such as lungs, intestines, kidneys and genitals all start to develop around weeks three to five. Around this time the face begins to take shape. Bumps on this tiny body grow into limbs, then fingers and toes are formed.

By week fourteen, the end of the first trimester, the foetus is only a little over 5 cm (2 in) from the top of its head to the bottom of the spine. Some of the major organs are completely formed, though extremely tiny, and the rest are still developing. The baby is already

THE PELVIC ORGANS

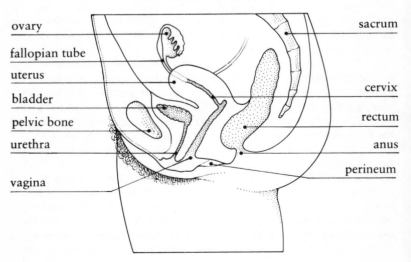

ovary

fallopian tube

uterus

bladder

pelvic bone

urethra

vagina

sacrum

cervix

rectum

anus

perineum

able to move in its liquid home, known as the amniotic sac. At this stage, although it is recognisably human, this tiny being could not live outside the womb. It takes virtually the next six months to grow and mature.

Action for You to Take

At about eight weeks, you should visit your GP. He or she will confirm your pregnancy and you will then be logged into the system of antenatal care in your area. These systems vary, but will be explained to you by your GP. You may go to the hospital for all your care or, more commonly, you may attend your first antenatal appointment at the hospital then see your midwife or GP until the final few weeks before the baby is due. Health visitors are often involved in antenatal care either for home visits or for giving classes.

Your First Antenatal Check

The first visit to the clinic will be at about twelve weeks and may be the most time-consuming. You will not only have to have a thorough check but also get all your details put on to the hospital records. Recently many hospitals have tried to reduce the waiting period, but it is best to be armed with something to do.

First, you will be weighed. You will then be weighed regularly throughout your pregnancy to keep a record of how this increases. A steady, controlled weight gain is best. Most women gain 9–12.5 kg (20–28 lb) during pregnancy, which includes not only the weight of the baby but also the placenta, womb and amniotic fluid, the increase in the size of your breasts, the larger volume of blood, and extra body fat which your body lays down as a reserve to supplement your diet while breast feeding.

Your blood pressure will be checked. This is also monitored throughout pregnancy in case of sudden ups or downs. If your blood pressure rises too high, this may be an indication of pre-eclampsia (see page 50) if you also have fluid retention and protein in the urine.

A blood sample will be taken so that your blood can be checked for a number of things.

Firstly, to check your blood group, as with any prospective hospital stay.

Secondly, to see whether you are rhesus negative. If you are, the hospital will need evidence of your partner's rhesus factor. If you are both rhesus negative, then the baby will also be negative and there will be no problem. If your partner is rhesus positive, then the baby could also be rhesus positive. A rhesus positive baby developing in a rhesus negative mother causes the mother's immune system to create antibodies in her blood. This is unlikely to be a problem with the current pregnancy unless these antibodies cross to the baby in very early pregnancy. However, they can harm a subsequent baby. The precaution the hospital will take is to give an injection (in most cases automatically) after the birth that prevents these antibodies developing in your bloodstream.

Thirdly, to check your immunity to rubella (see page 8).

Fourthly, to see if you are anaemic. If so, you may be prescribed iron tablets.

Finally, to see whether you have or have had syphilis or hepatitis B, both of which can be treated. In many hospitals, pregnant women are also tested for HIV because of the danger of the virus being passed on to the baby.

As well as blood tests, you will also need to give a sample of urine for testing so remember not to go to the lavatory just before the appointment. The doctor needs to check that there is no protein in your urine to show that your kidneys are coping with the extra waste products created by the baby. Protein in the urine can also be an indication of a urinary infection. If sugar is found in the urine on several occasions, this can be a sign of diabetes.

You may have an ultrasound scan at this appointment. This is a fascinating experience. It involves lying on a couch and baring your tummy which is then oiled. A hand-operated machine is passed over your skin. This bounces sound waves off your baby which are then translated into a picture on a television screen. If you have ultrasound even as early as nine or ten weeks, you may be able to see the heart beating. The hospital can measure the length of the foetus to check the expected date of arrival and see if the baby is growing normally. On later ultrasound scans, you can see the outline of your baby with perhaps its legs kicking. From personal experience I can assure you this is very exciting.

To have a successful ultrasound scan, you must have a full bladder. This requires you to drink at least 600 ml (2 pints) of liquid an hour or so beforehand. Holding on to this is probably the most uncomfortable part of the whole proceeding.

All this information is filled in on a card known as a co-operation card, which you should carry with you throughout your pregnancy. It will be updated at each antenatal visit either to the hospital or to your doctor.

You should also get a form FW8 which entitles you to free prescriptions. Tell your dentist, too, that you are expecting as you are allowed free dental treatment during pregnancy and for a year after the birth.

Your Developing Baby

Week 6

The embryo is 6mm ($\frac{1}{4}$in) long. It is beginning to develop a brain, spine and nervous system and the heart is now beating. Small buds are visible where the limbs are beginning to grow. There are signs of ears and eyes.

Week 8

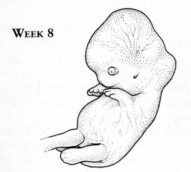

The embryo is 2.5cm (1in) long. It is now a fetus. Most of the internal organs are developing and externally the facial features are beginning to emerge. The fetus begins to move around.

Week 12

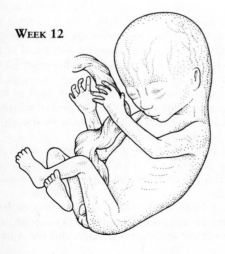

A key week in the development of your baby. The fetus is 6.5cm ($2\frac{1}{2}$in) long. The face has its eyes, nose and mouth, the fingers and toes are fully formed and have nails. The muscles are developing and the baby is able to suck, swallow the amniotic fluid and pass urine.

Extra Tests

For some women, the doctor may recommend an amniocentesis between fourteen and sixteen weeks. This involves taking a small amount of amniotic fluid for testing and can show up abnormalities such as Down's syndrome and spina bifida. Discuss this with your doctor if you want more information.

Twins

About one pregnancy in eighty results in twins. If more than one egg has been released at the same time by the ovaries and then fertilised, the twins will be fraternal. If a single egg divides after fertilisation, the twins will be identical. If twins are suspected, you may be offered an extra ultrasound scan as this is the easiest way to confirm the diagnosis, although in some cases this cannot be confirmed until almost half way through the pregnancy.

If you are expecting twins – or a multiple birth – you will be closely monitored by the doctor and may be advised additional rest because of the extra demands on your body. The chances of premature birth are higher with twins, and if you have not delivered by thirty-six or thirty-eight weeks you may be induced, as there is a risk that the placenta will start to break down. Because twins are usually smaller than a single baby, they may need to be kept in intensive care for a short time after the birth. Your doctor or midwife will discuss this with you as early as possible.

A Home Delivery

If you would like a home delivery, it is best to discuss this as soon as possible with your doctor or mention it on your first antenatal visit.

Some women feel that a home birth is preferable to hospital. They know they will feel happier and more relaxed in familiar surroundings. There's no need to worry about rushing off to the hospital once your labour starts. By being at home, you may avoid unnecessary medical intervention. It is also argued that there is less risk of infection. It is true, however, that 'high tech' won't be immediately on hand should there be an emergency. Although most districts do have a flying squad who can come quickly to your home or transfer you to hospital should the need arise, this may be a concern. If the safety of a home birth is an aspect that worries you, you should check on the availability of emergency help before making a decision. Some women have their first child in hospital and a subsequent child at home. This fits in with the first delivery being the longest and most unpredictable one.

Even if a home delivery is what you want, it may not always be possible. Medical conditions such as heart trouble may mean that you will need specialist monitoring which would not be possible at home. Your doctor will also consider other factors such as whether this is your first delivery, whether you have had complications in the past and how your present pregnancy is progressing. Even if you are likely to have a normal delivery your doctor may advise against a home delivery. Some doctors do not undertake them.

You don't need your doctor's agreement to have a home birth, however. Deliveries are undertaken by community midwives. To find out about these get in touch with the Supervisor of Midwives for your area. It may be necessary to write. She has a legal obligation to provide you with a midwife. She will need to know your due date. An alternative is to transfer to an obstetric GP who will then be involved in the birth, though she may not necessarily do the delivery herself.

If your baby is to be born at home, then towards the end of your pregnancy your midwife will leave a pack of sterile equipment with you so that it is ready when needed. She will also give you some idea of what you yourself will need to have ready.

When you go into labour you need to phone for the midwife. She will check how your labour is progressing and either stay or leave depending on how it's going. If she leaves she will tell you when she will return. Usually it is arranged for two midwives to be present for the birth itself. They stay afterwards until everything is cleared up and you and your new baby are settled. It is important that you organise proper domestic help after the birth and not be under the impression that because you have had the baby at home you'll be able to carry on as usual.

There are a number of home birth support groups (see useful addresses on page 170) and the National Childbirth Trust also publishes a booklet on home birth.

Mid Term

This is the part of your pregnancy from fifteen to twenty-eight weeks. It is often called the 'blooming' time.

What is Happening to You

Many women find the middle part of their pregnancy is a time when they really bloom. You are probably over the nausea and tiredness. At the beginning of this trimester, you may only have gained a small amount of extra weight. This means you can still get about easily and wear many of your ordinary clothes. During this period your bump will probably develop quite considerably, though it may not seem too cumbersome. This change can be exciting as you start to be aware of the baby and feel truly pregnant.

At around eighteen to twenty weeks, though much earlier for second mums, you may also feel your baby beginning to move. At first this may seem like a fluttering or bubbling sensation which you may confuse with your tummy rumbling! It then dawns on you that this is the baby. Those early flutters soon turn into more definite movements and you begin to be aware of your baby's waking and sleeping periods. These generally don't coincide with yours. Your partner may also be able to listen to your baby's heart beat. This is much faster than an adult heart rate. It can be hard to identify, but try using something such as a cardboard tube to amplify the sound.

My morning sickness disappeared during the second third of my pregnancy. I felt absolutely marvellous during this time. In contrast to the dreadful tiredness of the first phase, I felt I had extra energy. We went on a walking holiday in Scotland, and spent the long climbs uphill discussing names for the baby. Luckily all our favourite places had quite unpronounceable names. I couldn't quite envisage calling the baby Glomach. Apart from being on a physical high, this was a good period mentally too. I started to believe I was pregnant and found it very exciting as the bump began to show and my clothes no longer fitted. More exciting still were those first fluttering feelings inside. I didn't even mind that Ralph's liveliest time seemed to be just when I wanted to go to sleep. The odd nudge in the ribs became rather comforting.

What is Happening Inside

During this period, the baby continues to grow and by week twenty-eight will weigh about 1.25 kg (2½ lb). Those organs not completely formed in the first trimester develop fully. These include the spinal cord and brain, lungs and intestinal system.

During this trimester, the eyes develop fully and will move when the baby changes position. While still inside you, the baby can respond to bright or flashing lights visible through the skin and womb. The baby's ears and all the hearing apparatus are also complete. The baby can now hear both internal sounds such as your heart beat as well as reacting to loud noises outside the womb.

Some fine details begin to appear – facial features, such as eyebrows, eyelids and lashes, as well as toe and finger nails and finger prints. The baby can open and close its hands, has the ability to grip and may suck its thumb.

From about twenty-two weeks, the baby is covered in lanugo, a fine soft hair. This is thought to keep the baby at the right temperature. Most of this hair disappears before birth. At the end of this period, all the major organs are complete and the baby is considered viable. This means that there would be a chance of survival if it were born, although probably in most cases only a small chance and that with the help of intensive care.

YOUR BABY AT WEEK 20

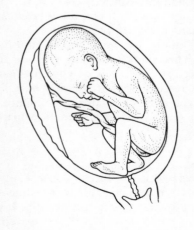

The fetus is 25cm (10in) long. You may now feel a light, fluttering sensation which is the fetus moving around. Some babies will be quieter than others but this is nothing to worry about. He will probably now be sensitive to external noises. Hair and teeth are beginning to appear.

Action for You to Take

You will probably be seen every four weeks during this trimester from sixteen weeks onwards. Depending on the system in your area, you may see your GP, the midwife or go to the hospital – or a combination of the three. In any event, you will have a urine test; your blood pressure will be checked; and your weight measured. Most doctors or midwives will also listen to the foetal heart beat.

In many areas, you will attend the hospital for a routine ultrasound scan at between sixteen and eighteen weeks. This time is chosen because it gives the most accurate assessment of the baby's growth rate.

Clothing

At some point during your second trimester you will probably have to adjust your wardrobe to accommodate your bump. Maternity wear has improved greatly and has lost much of its frumpy or twee look. Fashion, though, has changed too. There is a good choice now for mums-to-be in ordinary clothing that is designed to be loosely fitted. It is also worth looking at sizes larger than you would normally wear. Of the special maternity designs, I found maternity trousers very useful. They are made with expandable waistlines that can be altered as your size changes. You get a lot of wear from these from early on when you just need a little extra room around the waist to the last few weeks when you can be huge. Afterwards you can wear them while you get back in shape.

If you need to have something for a special occasion, you may be able to borrow something from a friend. If not, it can be cheaper to hire rather than buy, and many firms offer this service.

Depending on your size, another essential item to put on the shopping list is a good bra which fits comfortably and gives adequate support. You may find you need to buy a few as your pregnancy advances and you gradually increase in size, or you may be able to buy one that will adjust to fit you during the later stages. Once the baby is born you may need a nursing bra. More information on these on page 44.

Maternity Rights

It is best to contact your local social security office or Citizens Advice Bureau as there are a variety of benefits available to working and non-working parents, according to a range of circumstances. If you are working, week twenty-nine is the earliest you can take maternity leave. In order to get maternity pay you need to give three weeks' notice. During week twenty-six you will need to inform your employer if you want to stop at the earliest opportunity. Your employer will also need to know when the baby is due and whether you intend going back. Week thirty-four is the latest you can stop and still get eighteen weeks Statutory Maternity Pay (SMP) or Maternity Allowance. It is also worth checking on what benefits are available after the baby is born such as child or one-parent benefit.

Antenatal Classes

Decide about and book antenatal classes during this period as some classes fill quickly. Classes will be run by a GP clinic, your hospital or by private groups such as the National Childbirth Trust. GP and hospital classes are free. You may be offered a series of general classes (usually six classes) or a specific class for a topic such as breast feeding. General classes aim to cover all aspects of labour, birth and how to look after your new born baby.

If you can find the time and energy, attending antenatal classes is very worthwhile. It puts you in the position of knowing what options are available and why. If you are working you may have a right to have paid time off to attend these classes as part of your antenatal appointments.

You can learn about the stages of pregnancy, how to recognise labour when it starts and what to do. You will learn about the stages of labour and birth. Methods of pain relief will be discussed, with explanations about drugs or procedures which may be used in labour. There might be explanations of terms used such as episiotomy (a cut made in the perineum to enable the baby's head to come out more easily, reputedly the most common operation in Britain). Breathing techniques and positions for birth are usually discussed and practised. You may be given exercises for before and after, and advice on recovery. You'll probably be given guidelines on what you will need in hospital, what the baby needs, and the pros and cons of breast and bottle feeding.

Classes help to take away some of the mystery (not the miracle) of birth. They can make you aware of many of the possibilities open to you, so at least when you do have to make choices you have some knowledge on which to base your decisions. Either for routine or important things, it gives you a chance to think about them beforehand. There is often time to discuss worries which you might not always manage to bring up at your antenatal appointments.

Partners are often welcomed at these classes so they too can understand what is going on and learn about the role they might play at the birth.

Hospital Classes

These are usually organised by the hospital midwives with other members of staff, such as the physiotherapist, giving advice. As well as covering the subjects mentioned above, you will probably be offered a tour of the hospital. Although you may feel that one ward is very like another, your hospital may be divided into labour wards, delivery suites, reception room, maternity ward and so on. Getting a sense of the geography and relation between all these things can help you feel more at home when you arrive. I was sorry that I missed my hospital tour as I felt in retrospect I would have felt more at ease from the start if the surroundings had been a little more familiar. Hospital classes may also introduce you to the different staff you might meet and explain about the system of looking after you once you go into labour. Take the opportunity to find out about all the facilities available. The hospital may have bean bags which many people find comfortable in labour, or they may have a 'low tech' delivery room designed for mothers who find the paraphernalia of normal delivery rooms a little daunting.

Looking round the hospital will also give you a chance to ask about the food on offer and have a look at the menus. If you are vegetarian you can ask and see what sort of food is provided for vegetarians.

National Childbirth Trust Classes

The National Childbirth Trust (NCT) is a charity that runs antenatal classes for which there is usually a fee. The NCT trains its own teachers for these classes. These teachers are all mothers. Although the classes are broadly the same, they will differ slightly according to the teacher and the individuals that make up the group. Classes are generally held in the teacher's home. Some are for mothers, with one evening which the fathers also attend, but some are for couples.

The classes will cover the topics mentioned above. More emphasis may be put on active birth – that is how you can make a positive contribution to the birth. NCT classes may also discuss alternative therapies for labour, such as acupuncture and yoga.

A plus point of NCT classes is that they are usually small and run very informally. Members of the group have a chance to get to know each other. They are encouraged to stay in touch afterwards and provide a valuable network of support both before and afterwards. With my own group, we had a postnatal reunion, followed by regular meetings as the year went on. It seemed no time at all when the first birthday party invitations started arriving.

The Third Trimester

This is the last three months, from week twenty-nine to the birth — you will be growing bigger and bigger.

What is Happening to You

During the last part of your pregnancy, you will probably both feel and look really pregnant, especially towards the end. It is not only the bump that is growing but your breasts too will increase in size. You should be able to feel the baby move quite strongly, certainly in the early part of the trimester. As his size increases he has less room to move, though movement there is nevertheless.

As this trimester progresses, you will be aware of the extra weight you are carrying and probably feel increasingly tired. If you can, try to get some rest during the day. This is easier if it is your first baby as you have only yourself to look after. The more rested you are before the birth the better you will cope with that, and the better able you will be to handle the inevitable tiredness later.

Towards the end of your pregnancy, you may have difficulty sleeping as, apart from more trips to the loo, your extra weight makes it hard to get comfortable. It can help if you can get masses of pillows to prop around you to give you more support. Water beds are popular in the United States with some women at this stage of their pregnancy! If you can't sleep, try to keep relaxed rather than tossing and turning. Reading or listening to tapes may help, or try a soothing bedtime drink such as a herbal tea. Practise the relaxation techniques you have learnt at your antenatal classes.

During these last weeks you may also find yourself needing to nip to the loo more often. This is because the baby crowds things somewhat, and your bladder notices. The baby may at some point turn and drop down into the pelvis, which squashes the bladder even more. Compensation may come from there being more room for your stomach. If you have suffered from heartburn and indigestion, this may ease and you'll be able to eat bigger meals.

I had mixed feelings about the last few weeks of my own pregnancy. At first my energy and sense of well-being carried over into the final part. I still didn't feel as though I was carrying a huge amount of extra weight although I definitely looked pregnant. I busied myself with antenatal classes run by both the National Child-birth Trust and the hospital. By the time the eighth month arrived, my increased weight, the incredibly hot summer weather and my inability to sleep well got the better of me. I was very grateful for 'talking books' which I went through at a terrific rate in hours of night-time listening. The heat made me feel like a beached whale. I sat in cool baths at two o'clock in the morning and even resorted to pinching the ice packs from the picnic box to try to cool down my feet. I had never thought the day would come when I could balance a plate of sandwiches quite comfortably on my tummy and decided to have a photo to remind me how enormous I had suddenly become.

One unexpected side effect of the latter stages of pregnancy was a new buoyancy I had in the water which made swimming great fun. I discovered that the extra weight acted like a float so I could bob up and down quite happily in the sea. On the plus side too is the feeling that the baby will soon arrive. I had all the nesting feelings common at this time. This led to several moves of furniture and frantic DIY sessions plus late night shopping trips to lay in a stock of goodies.

What is Happening Inside

From week twenty-eight the baby still needs to grow considerably to survive without help, and he now does so quickly. He puts on roughly 200 g (7 oz) a week up until the birth. His skin, which was rather wrinkled, now fills out so that by forty weeks it is almost smooth. The skin is covered with a thick grease called 'vernix' which is thought to protect it from the surrounding fluid in the womb. It's a bit like the preparation cross-Channel swimmers make so they do not get waterlogged. By birth both the vernix and all or most of the lanugo disappears.

Around week thirty-two, the baby may well turn upside down in order to be in the right position for birth. Some don't turn until the last week or so, but only about 10 per cent don't turn round at all. When a baby is born feet first, it is called a breech birth. In some cases, these babies can be delivered vaginally, otherwise a Caesarean is needed (see page 67). When the baby's head sinks into the pelvis, this is known technically as being engaged. It may be written on your notes as 1/5, meaning the baby is one fifth of the way down.

Action for You to Take

During this time there are several things it is wise to think about and get ready. It is probably better to be prepared earlier rather than later as towards the end of your pregnancy your mobility and your energy

YOUR BABY AT WEEK 32

The fetus is 40.5cm (16in). By this stage most first babies have turned upside down ready for birth, although this does vary. Some won't turn until the start of labour. The baby's proportions are as they will be at birth, but he is still gaining weight.

may decrease. The baby may also be early. Now is the time to think about minimising the work when you come home with the baby by laying in stocks of easy to prepare food. You must also check that you have everything you will need for the baby, and pack your bags for the hospital so that you can be off at a moment's notice. Work out your travel arrangements to the hospital and keep a list of telephone numbers (labour ward, antenatal clinic, doctor etc) in your handbag or diary and stuck to the telephone.

Food Stocks

If your circumstances are such that you want to lay in stocks of food, now is the time. Fill your cupboards and freezer with items that will be useful after the baby arrives. The thought of bulk cooking may be too daunting. Instead you could simply cook double quantities regularly and put the remaining portions away in the freezer. If you haven't the energy to cook, then at least try to get one or two bulk shopping trips done so you won't have to buy too much heavyweight stuff for some time afterwards. An advantage of many vegetarian staples is their long shelf life. Here is a check list of items you might get in stock.

The following should last up to six months:
- porridge oats
- breakfast cereals such as muesli
- nuts and seeds including almonds, cashews, walnuts
- nut and seed butters such as peanut butter and tahini
- flour (best used within three months)
- concentrated apple juice
- soya milk
- selection of whole grains such as rice, buckwheat and bulgar wheat

The following should last a year (tinned products longer):
- selection of dried fruit
- dried pasta
- lentils
- tinned pulses
- tinned baked beans
- tinned tomatoes
- tomato purée
- olive oil
- sunflower oil
- shoyu (soy sauce)
- mineral water

Non-food items to stock up on include:
- washing powder
- fabric conditioner
- loo rolls
- kitchen rolls
- household cleaning products

Buying for the Baby

This is also a good time to do some preparation for the baby. There are often guidelines in the shops showing what you need for your baby initially. It is easy to spend more money than necessary, which is why it is a useful idea to have a good look round first and take time to make your mind up on what to buy. Remember that babies are big business. There is an enormous amount on the market that we are made to feel we must use, but much of it is quite unnecessary. With something like nappy changing, plain warm water, cotton wool, adequate drying, and vaseline will do just as well as antiseptic wipes and creams.

You may wish to buy products that have not been tested on animals and are environmentally friendly. Many readily available brands are marked as such, and there are also specialist shops that sell cruelty-free baby care products such as shampoo, baby bath and barrier creams. If you can't find a particular product that has not been tested on animals, it may be worth seeing if you need it anyway.

Concern for the environment may influence your decision on nappies. In Britain, some 3.5 billion disposables are used each year which represents about seven million trees. Disposable nappies are certainly extremely convenient, but they are only disposable as far as your own dustbin. Unfortunately the 80 tons or so of nappies that are dumped every hour in Britain are rapidly filling landfill sites. You may prefer to use ordinary terry towelling nappies which need folding. You can also buy more expensive pre-folded pure wool or cotton nappies which can be re-used. For more information on nappies and the environment, contact The Women's Environmental Network (information on page 169). They also have a list of suppliers of non-disposable nappies and nappy washing services.

Essential Items for the Baby

This list includes just the bare essentials for the new baby:
- two dozen re-usable towelling nappies plus one-way liners or one packet smallest size disposable nappies;
- four vests or body suits;
- four stretch suits or two stretch suits and two nighties plus socks or bootees;
- two cardigans or jackets;
- a shawl or blanket;
- cotton wool, tissues, barrier cream

If you bottle feed you will need:
- six bottles and teats;
- sterilising equipment;
- a bottle brush
- a supply of vegetarian baby milk

The baby obviously needs somewhere to sleep. New born babies tend not to start off in a cot as it can be too big. A carry cot that converts to a pram can be good value as the baby can sleep in this up to about three months. Special first cradles and Moses baskets are also available. Three sheets are needed for the bedding, with two or three blankets, depending on the time of year. Baby size duvets are available but you may decide against these because of the risk of over heating.

You also need a way of transporting the baby. New babies should travel flat as their back muscles aren't strong enough to support them. Some pushchairs will recline this far and with the addition of padding can make a flat base. Otherwise buy a traditional pram, or carrycot and pushchair combination. The very lightweight buggies that fold up like umbrellas are only suitable for babies once they are over six months old.

In the car, carry cot restraints often have to be specially fitted but do mean that you can transport the baby safely. If you use a carry cot in the car, remember that the baby must be strapped into the carry cot, as well as strapping the carry cot into the car. Numerous baby carriers are also available. These are fitted using ordinary seat belts. Some garages offer a free or low-cost fitting service for cot restraints or straps and car seats. It may be worth enquiring locally.

Nursing Bras

If you have not already bought a good bra for yourself, you will need to buy one now, remembering that you will probably get bigger towards the end of the pregnancy. You will also need at least one nursing bra if you are intending to breast feed, and it is best to buy this at about thirty-four weeks. It is worth getting fitted for a proper bra by a specialist shop or by the Mava agent from the NCT. You will need a bra that will give you good support, be easy to undo with one hand, support the breast which is not feeding and not constrict your breasts. Avoid nursing bras with a circle of fabric around the breast and a flap over the top as these can cause constriction.

Your Hospital Bags

You should be given advice by the hospital and at your classes on what to bring in with you, as provisions vary from region to region. Quantities depend on your intended length of stay, but if you take in enough to cover the first twenty-four hours or so, your partner can always bring in more supplies as necessary.

You should pack separately the things you will need in the labour ward and the things you will need on the postnatal ward. Your 'labour' nightie will not be much use if it is buried under breast pads and bags of nappies.

Labour Bag
- an old nightdress or T-shirt to wear in labour
- a natural sponge and/or natural water spray for if you get hot during labour
- a hot water bottle and cover and/or socks in case you get cold during labour
- jigsaw/cards/Walkman for using up time in labour

- telephone card or money
- list of telephone numbers
- flask of tea/coffee or cold drinks for partner
- snack foods for partner
- camera and film
- co-operation card

Hospital Bag

- nightdress or equivalent: front opening if you intend to breast feed
- dressing gown
- slippers
- nursing bras
- sponge bag containing flannel, hairbrush, toothbrush etc
- towel
- hair dryer (although check with the hospital as some will not allow you to take in any electrical equipment)
- breast pads in case you leak milk
- soft extra absorbent sanitary pads
- pants, belt or NCT stretch briefs to hold these in place
- tissues
- loose clothing to wear afterwards
- notebook, writing paper, address book and pen
- birth announcement cards and stamps
- books or magazines
- cereal and biscuits
- juice and/or mineral water

Baby's Bag

Many hospitals supply clothing for the baby, although others expect you to take your own. The baby's first motions are very runny, so take at least two of each item of clothing. Some hospitals expect you to take in two small margarine tubs for 'topping and tailing' (washing the face and bottom) the baby. You may also need to take in your own towels.

- vests
- all-in-one baby suits or nighties and booties
- shawl
- jacket and hat if it is cold
- nappies and barrier cream
- tissues and cotton wool

Common Complaints During Pregnancy

Although it would be ideal if we could all follow the advice given in the section on how to have a healthy diet, sometimes your body just won't let you. For example, if you suffer from nausea in the first few months of pregnancy you may not be able to face food at all or have a craving for junk foods that you normally wouldn't want. This point emphasises the need to try and be well nourished in the first place.

There are several complaints, such as cramp or nausea, that are quite common in pregnancy. Whilst they are not likely to be life threatening they are unpleasant. This chapter looks at some of those complaints, and suggests some changes in your diet that may help to ease them.

Anaemia

During pregnancy, the volume of blood in the body increases. This can lead to a drop in the blood's haemoglobin level, that is the proportion of the blood that is the red, oxygen carrying cells. If this level is too low you are said to be anaemic. This is a common condition in pregnancy. If you become anaemic, your heart has to do more work to keep your baby supplied with oxygen. To provide the same amount of oxygen means more blood which needs more pumping. You may feel more tired more easily (you could feel that anyway, of course). You are less likely to be able to cope easily with the loss of blood during labour.

The body requires iron to make red blood cells, and more iron is the usual way of addressing anaemia. Iron tablets may be offered, but they can have side effects so I think it is desirable to have plenty of iron in your diet.

Anaemia seems to be one of the principle worries the medical profession has about vegetarian mothers-to-be. This is because the traditional sources of iron are contained in meat, liver and seafood. Yet iron is also available in many foods vegetarians will eat including egg yolks, blackstrap molasses, dried fruits such as peaches, apricots and figs, wheatgerm and pulses, particularly lentils.

In addition to lack of iron causing anaemia, it is thought that deficiency in other nutrients, such as protein and folic acid, can contribute. To obtain sufficient protein, make sure you have combinations of cereals, nuts or pulses. Sources of folic acid include grains, bread, nuts and green vegetables.

Remember to eat plenty of vitamin C in order to increase your absorption of iron.

There is more information on nutrients on page 11.

Bleeding Gums

Due to hormonal changes when you are pregnant, it is not unusual to have mild gum disease. The gums may feel tender, be a little swollen and may have a tendency to bleed more easily. You can help the condition by cleaning your teeth thoroughly and regularly. Invest in a new toothbrush. Also use floss regularly.

From a diet point of view try to avoid eating too much sugar, especially as snacks between meals. If you feel hungry, choose fresh fruit or bread or toast with a savoury spread.

Breathlessness

Especially as your pregnancy advances, you may find that you suffer increasingly from breathlessness after any slight exertion. This is caused by the pressure of the growing baby up on to the lower lungs, and also the movement of blood away from the lungs to the growing womb. If you find this a problem, you will need to take things a bit easier.

Constipation

This is common in early pregnancy due to those hormonal changes. In later pregnancy too, your system can also get a bit sluggish as the ligaments relax and soften.

As a vegetarian, you will probably be eating plenty of fibre in foods such as brown rice, wholemeal bread and pulses. If you suffer from constipation try increasing the amount of liquid you drink each day.

Cramp

Cramp can come on and off during pregnancy. It usually happens in the lower legs and often at night, which is unfortunate if you have just fallen asleep.

The cause of cramp isn't definitely known. Some nutritionists attribute it to too little calcium, others to too much and an imbalance between calcium and magnesium. Low salt diets have also been blamed for causing cramp.

You may need to experiment with your diet to see if you can ease the problem. If you need to increase your calcium intake and can tolerate dairy produce, eat more yoghurt, cheese and drink milk. Remember to choose the low fat varieties. Also eat tofu and soya milk products, checking they are calcium enriched. For more information on calcium, see page 17.

If you have too much calcium and therefore a need for more magnesium, obtain this from eating leafy vegetables.

If you have a very low salt diet, you can start adding very small quantities of ordinary salt to your food. If this is going to ruin the flavour, try using more shoyu which does contain salt.

Apart from making changes to your diet, exercise may help as this will stimulate your circulation. Just before you go to bed, try flexing and pointing your toes, and circling your ankles.

Indigestion and Heartburn

You may find that certain foods you have previously enjoyed give you indigestion during pregnancy. You probably can't predict which ones, although tea, coffee and spicy foods are common culprits. All you can do is give these up for the time being.

Heartburn is different from indigestion. This can become more common later in pregnancy when the baby inside has grown so big that the uterus starts to press on the stomach. The muscle between the oesophagus and the stomach relaxes. The enlarged uterus pushes acid from the stomach upwards and causes a burning sensation in the chest.

There is no one special food that will help or should be avoided except perhaps spicy foods. One possible remedy is to try eating several small meals rather than three large ones, as this means your stomach shouldn't become so full. When you do eat, whether snacking or proper meals, try to sit up very straight. This helps to make more room for everything going on inside.

Nausea or Morning Sickness

Morning sickness is thought to be caused by the hormonal changes going on in your body. You can see in the chapter on the early development of the foetus what an enormous amount is happening, particularly in the first few weeks.

Although it is called morning sickness, it isn't exclusively a morning feeling. The nausea can be felt at any time of the day, or in some cases last from morning till night. It can be as bad as actually being physically sick, or can mean you have a funny taste in your mouth, or a faint feeling. Certain foods, either eating them or merely thinking about them, can make you feel bad. Going off tea or coffee is very common. Nausea is probably the main thing that will prevent you eating properly despite your good intentions to have an excellent diet.

Usually the worst of the sick feelings disappear around weeks fourteen to sixteen, though some women are unfortunate enough to suffer from nausea throughout pregnancy. The good news is that you can do a few things to help yourself feel better.

You may feel worst in the morning. If this is the case, try to eat something plain before you get up. Something like a plain biscuit, dry toast or a rice cake can help. It may not be quite the luxury breakfast in bed you think you deserve, but it will ease you into the day. If you have gone off tea or coffee, find a herbal tea, such as a lemon verbena, that will cleanse or refresh you.

It may also help if you can prevent yourself from getting too hungry, as hunger can make nausea worse. Try not to skip meals. If your normal routine is to have three meals, you may find it better to eat several small snacks. If you are at work you could take with you a sandwich, rice cakes spread with a nut butter, a bag of dried fruit and nuts, a piece of fresh fruit. If you were at home you could have a bowl of soup, a baked potato with cottage cheese, silken tofu blended with banana and wheatgerm. Try to keep the snacks nutritious.

Nausea can also be brought on by certain foods or smells. It is sensible to avoid these if you can. From a nutritional point of view, there is usually a suitable alternative. If you can't face milk, for instance, you can get calcium from other sources such as enriched soya milk.

It is not always a bad thing to respond to your cravings. This may well contradict some of the above advice! I needed to have something sweet at around eleven o'clock in the morning. I fought this at first, being conscious that sugar wasn't going to do my diet much good. But I found that I did feel better once I succumbed to the odd chocolate biscuit snack. Once the sickness had gone I was able to drop the habit. If you do have a craving for something you know is rather unhealthy, try to make sure the rest of your diet is as good as you can make it.

There are also some herbal remedies that can help ease nausea. Ginger tea is an old remedy for travel sickness which can also help to reduce nausea. Fennel tea aids digestion and seems to cleanse the palate. Lemon verbena also has a cleansing effect on the palate, and chamomile tea is a remedy both for nausea (and hangovers!).

Oedema

Slight swelling of the ankles, feet and fingers is common in pregnancy because of extra fluid retained by the body. The doctor will monitor this carefully in case it is an indication of pre-eclampsia (see below). If you get this condition try to rest and relax a little more. A useful remedy is to try lying on your back with your feet resting against a wall. Later on in pregnancy, during the last two to three months, lying on your back can restrict circulation and you may feel faint. You can still do this exercise but not for more than five minutes. Stop immediately if you feel any discomfort.

Passing Water

Needing to go to the lavatory more frequently is a hazard of pregnancy. Don't give up drinking because of it! You do need extra liquid both to help avoid constipation and because of the increased volume of blood in your body. Before going out always remember to have an extra pee even if you don't feel you need it.

Piles

These can be caused during pregnancy by straining if you can't pass a motion. The best approach is not to get constipated by taking the dietary advice above, including maintaining your liquid intake. But this may not be completely successful. If you do get piles there are creams and homoeopathic remedies available from the chemist that can help.

After the baby is born, you may also get piles due to the pushing in the second stage of labour. Most teaching about this stage says the pushing is rather like straining to go to the loo. Some teachers will try and help you visualise an opening up sensation rather than concentrate on the pushing side. It might be worth discussing this at your antenatal class.

Pre-Eclampsia

Pre-eclampsia, or toxaemia, is a less common condition which can occur towards the end of pregnancy. The cause is not definitely known, although it basically indicates that the kidneys are not coping with the extra waste products from the baby. The symptoms are high blood pressure, oedema and protein in the urine. Because this can quickly progress to severe pre-eclampsia, in which case the kidneys could be permanently damaged, any women showing these symptoms will be ordered to rest, possibly in hospital, so that their blood pressure and urine can be closely monitored until the baby is born. After delivery, the signs quickly disappear.

Vaginal Discharge

Nearly all women have more vaginal discharge during pregnancy. Generally this is nothing to worry about. If you are sore or itchy, however, this may be an infection such as thrush. Pessaries can be prescribed by the doctor for this condition. A good deal of faith is put into eating natural yoghurt which helps fight the yeast responsible for the infection. If the discharge contains any blood you should also tell your doctor or go to the clinic for advice.

Varicose Veins

These are caused when the blood flowing back from your legs to your heart is obstructed for a prolonged time. The blood then has to find a different route and uses the smaller veins closer to the surface of the skin. These then swell and show on the leg.

Try to avoid standing for long periods. Also try to avoid getting constipated (see page 47). Regular exercise can help prevent the problem. If you do suffer from varicose veins, make sure you sit down with your feet up for a short time each day, and consult your doctor at your next antenatal visit.

Alternative Treatments

This chapter will introduce you to some alternative forms of health care that you may find useful. Space doesn't allow me to go into much detail, but I have given contact addresses on page 170 if you would like more information.

Once you are pregnant you are going to see quite a bit of various people involved in the medical world – regardless of how you feel! There will probably be regular visits to your doctor and to several hospital staff, perhaps as many as ten or a dozen during the course of the pregnancy. If you have been unused to going regularly to the doctor or had only rare trips to hospital, this may feel a little unusual. You can feel you are constantly beating at the door of the various medical practitioners.

You are bound to be more conscious of your body because of all the changes occurring, and however carefully you look after yourself, physically and mentally, by trying to eat well and by exercising, it may be that you will suffer some of the common complaints of pregnancy. You may simply have days where you feel worn out or deflated. This shouldn't worry you, but you may like to do something about them. More visits to your doctor may not be appropriate. You could ask the opinion of a pharmacist or you could try an alternative therapy.

There are a variety of alternative therapies that you may find useful. These don't involve the use of drugs and are generally non-invasive. In this chapter, I've given a short description of some of the better known and an explanation of how they might be useful. They are relevant antenatally, during labour and in helping you recover after the birth. In some cases they can be useful for the baby. If you do consult anyone be sure to tell them that you are pregnant.

Acupuncture

Acupuncture is an ancient Chinese therapy that has been practised for over 5000 years. The basic principle is the belief that energy flows through numerous channels in the body. If the flow is blocked, interrupted or unbalanced, pain or illness can occur. Along these meridians, or energy lines, there are some 800 specific points which are thought to affect particular areas of the body or internal organs.

An acupuncturist is trained to tell which points need to be worked on in order to treat conditions.

To diagnose a disorder, an acupuncturist will feel the pulses in the body, twelve in all, six on each wrist. These pulses relate to the meridians of the body reflecting both the quality and quantity of energy. The state of the pulses helps determine the points that need to be treated. These points are worked on to rebalance the body's energy and to stimulate the body's own healing mechanism. Very fine needles are used on the point either alone or in conjunction with moxa bustion, a Chinese herb. This herb has been dried and moulded into a cone which is then burnt to heat the acupuncture point for extra stimulation or can be used in a compressed roll. Sometimes moxa is used alone without the needles. The amount of time the needles are left in place varies according to the treatment. Once you have undergone a successful course of treatment, the acupuncturist may suggest you return once every three months for a general session, rather like a car going in for a service!

Acupuncture can help disorders during pregnancy such as morning sickness. It can also be used during labour, both to help you cope with the pain of contractions and to help stimulate contractions (if for some reason these have started then stopped). Acupuncture has also been used to stimulate labour when the baby is overdue.

After having the baby, acupuncture may assist with general physical recovery, helping you to restore your energy levels. It can also be a way of treating individual disorders, such as migraine, that may occur after the birth.

If you think acupuncture could be useful for you, it is best to get in touch with an acupuncturist before getting pregnant. You might have an initial treatment simply to get your energy levels and bodily functions in good condition. It is important that the acupuncturist has some idea of your pulse readings before you conceive. Once you are pregnant these pulses change dramatically, which makes further diagnosis difficult. For this reason, an acupuncturist might be reluctant to take on a new patient who is already pregnant.

Aromatherapy or Essential Oils

Aromatherapy using essential oils was first practised by the Egyptians thousands of years ago. In the last century it was a popular therapy in France and it more recently became better known in Britain. As a therapy it is said to be particularly good for skin problems and for stress-related disorders. The essential oils used are extracted from flowers, herbs and trees. During a session with an aromatherapist, your individual case would be discussed. The therapist would then make up a suitable blend of oils to help your condition. These oils would be used for a specific massage (for a condition such as constipation) or for a general therapeutic massage in the case of stress. Following the treatment, you might be given a blend of oils to use for massage at home, or to put drops in the bath.

Essential oils can be used to to help problems which can occur in pregnancy such as stretch marks, nausea, backache and swollen legs and ankles. Aromatherapists also feel that babies born to mothers receiving regular massage with soothing oils may be more peaceful when born. After the birth, aromatherapy may be useful if you suffer depression or baby blues. It can also help with conditions such as cracked nipples (though this must be in conjunction with positioning the baby properly when breast feeding).

Whilst essential oils can easily be used at home, it is important to get professional advice when you are pregnant. This is because some oils can be harmful. Laxative oils, for example, might cause abdominal contractions.

Essential oils should not be used on babies under the age of one as they are too strong for their delicate skin. With some conditions, for example a blocked nose, you might be able to heat a little oil in a special burner which could then be used in a younger baby's room. In order to find out about aromatherapists you should contact the International Federation of Aromatherapists who publish a geographical list of practitioners (see page 171).

Flower Remedies

Thirty-eight different flower essences were discovered by Dr Bach to help different states of mind such as fear, anxiety or irritation. The principle of this therapy is that imbalance in our emotional and mental state is a reflection of ill health in our physical body. The emotions are therefore treated so that when mental health is restored, physical health should also return.

In its simplest form, it is a technique that can be applied by oneself, it merely being necessary to identify your emotional state. For more complex emotional states it is best to find out more about the subtleties of the therapy from specific books or from an alternative therapy centre, where there may be a counsellor specialising in the technique.

There are various essences that may well help you through pregnancy and later help your baby. Although it is possible to do self-diagnosis, there are two very useful all-purpose combinations, one a cream and one in drop form. These are particularly useful for any sort of trauma or shock.

Homoeopathy

Homoeopathy is the medical practice of treating like with like. It is essentially a natural healing process providing remedies to assist the patient regain health by stimulating the body's natural forces of recovery. It concentrates on treating the patient rather than the disease. Homoeopathy was practised by the Ancient Greeks. Today it is formally accepted as a safe and effective alternative form of medical treatment.

One of the principles of homoeopathic treatment is that individuals will vary in their response to an illness according to their temperament. Different people may therefore be prescribed different remedies for the same illness. There are, however, certain substances within homoeopathy known as 'specifics'. These substances can be used universally as they have a specific therapeutic action on certain ailments. Arnica is a good example: it is the standard treatment for bruises.

Specific homoeopathic remedies may well help you in pregnancy and after childbirth. There are also remedies, such as teething granules, that may help your baby. For specific pregnancy problems such as varicose veins, constipation and morning sickness, it is essential to go to a homoeopathic doctor who can assess you individually. You could also discuss your condition with a helpful pharmacist, many of whom now have an understanding of homoeopathy.

Reflexology

The ancient healing art of reflexology has been known for thousands of years. It was developed in the West in this century following research by a German, Dr Cornelius and then taken further by an American surgeon, William Fitzgerald. He observed that pressure on certain areas of the body could have an anaesthetising effect on a related area. He classified the body into ten vertical zones ending with the fingers and toes, and established a link between a specific reflex zone on the foot and areas and organs of the body. The foot is seen as a reflection of the whole body, and treating the foot can have a relaxing and healing effect on the whole body.

A reflexologist examines the feet, looking for areas of tension or blockages. Using gentle pressure applied by hand, the reflexologist will try to release any tension, restore the free flow of energy and allow the body to function to its optimum. Many trained reflexologists have a medical background. Several are midwives who have a detailed understanding of the process of pregnancy and labour.

As with acupuncture, it may be best to go to a reflexologist whilst you are planning to become pregnant. They may be able to improve your general well-being with an initial treatment, and also gain knowledge for use should you become pregnant. Some reflexologists will not take on a new patient in the first three months of a pregnancy.

Reflexology has been used to treat some of the common complaints of pregnancy such as constipation, nausea and indigestion. Treatments may also prevent you suffering urinary infections, diabetes or high blood pressure.

Reflexology may also be used in labour. During this time, the pelvic area needs to relax. The pain of contractions can make you tighten up more than relax. Reflexology may help release this tension, which in turn may make the birth process carry on more easily.

Postnatally, reflexology has been used to help the healing processes by taking down the swelling, stimulating endorphins which are part of the body's natural pain relief, and restoring a hormonal balance. It may help with lactation and sometimes with postnatal depression.

If you wish to have a reflexologist present at the birth of your baby, it is important to discuss this with your hospital or midwife. Reactions may vary, as although reflexology is practised by medically qualified people it is not scientifically understood.

TNS

Transcutaneous nerve stimulation – TNS for short – is a non-invasive method of pain relief. The process works by passing tiny electrical impulses through the skin. These stimulate the nerve fibres, blocking out some of the pain messages travelling to the brain. As fewer pain messages reach the brain, less pain is felt. This process also stimulates the body to produce some of its own pain relieving substances called endorphins and enkephalins.

This may all sound very modern, but in fact electricity has been used in medicine since AD 46. Interest was revived in the 1960s and in the 1980s studies were made on this type of pain relief in labour. It seemed that the majority of patients questioned found TNS useful and would use it again. So far, there is no evidence to show any ill effects on the baby.

The TNS machine uses four electrodes placed on the back, on either side of the spine at the point where the nerves from the uterus join the spinal cord. Thin leads connect these electrodes to a battery-powered stimulator which varies the strength and frequency of the impulses. When the TNS machine is operating you may feel a sort of tingling sensation.

As this form of pain relief has become more popular, some hospitals or GP surgeries offer demonstrations on how to use the machine and may well be able to supply you with one. It is also possible to hire a machine for a month around the time your baby is due. If you decide to do this, ask to be shown how to use the machine at one of your classes or hospital visits. This gives you time to familiarise yourself with the way it works.

I used a rental scheme to hire a TNS machine for my own labour. It did seem to lessen the pain in the early stages in conjunction with breathing and relaxation techniques. I particularly remember the journey to the hospital in the taxi where I felt able to cope with quite strong contractions.

Traditional Chinese Medicine

In China, traditional medicine using herbs is as well known as acupuncture, but that is not so far the case in the West. The two techniques are often used together in China, though both can be used separately. This applies equally in pregnancy. There are herbal remedies that can help with some of the common complaints of pregnancy such as morning sickness or high blood pressure. Problems such as mastitis may be eased with herbal medicine. There are also practitioners who have helped complaints in babies, such as cases of eczema. If you are interested in Chinese medicine, you should go to a trained practitioner. You should also inform your GP.

Yoga

Yoga is perhaps accurately classified as a discipline, rather than a therapy. The name is from the Sanskrit language; meaning yoke and refers to a union of the mind and the physical being. It is a system of philosophic meditation that promotes self-awareness and well-being. Yoga involves awareness of breathing and heartbeat, and exercise for both body and mind.

In pregnancy yoga can be beneficial for several reasons. On a superficial level, there are exercises that can keep you fit and improve or maintain your posture. This aspect of yoga makes you feel good physically, which often means you feel good mentally too. Exercises or postures learnt are useful for identifying areas of stiffness or tension in the body. You learn to concentrate on these areas and then use breathing techniques to help release tension and keep the joints supple. Stretching should never be forced, nor should it be a competition with anyone else.

Keeping your body supple during pregnancy and learning to release tension is very useful, as it will mean you are less prone to tiredness or lack of energy. Suppleness and bodily awareness may also help during childbirth. You may be able to adopt postures which help to make birth easier. There are also specific postures that can help some of the common ailments in pregnancy such as backache.

Controlled breathing is an essential part of yoga. Deep breathing techniques help keep the blood well oxygenated, improve circulation and help with relaxation – all things which are good for anyone who is pregnant.

The gentle approach of yoga can be ideal for those who have not exercised since childhood, as well as for those who are fit. The physical confidence you gain through learning the postures can give you a mental confidence which helps you cope with the stresses of pregnancy and labour.

A lot of yoga classes can be found. They are often run by local authorities or sports centres. There are yoga teachers who have a particular interest in yoga for pregnant women. Some of these teachers can be contacted through the Active Birth Movement (see page 169).

If you join a yoga class, it is essential that you tell the teacher you are pregnant.

Labour and Birth

Doubtless you know something of this already! It is very emotional and very exciting, and so everyone who has given birth remembers the event well. So, perhaps with some encouragement, they will talk about it. By all means listen and discuss, but I don't think you should expect any experience of yours to be the same. Labour and birth are different for everyone. The advice I best remember and feel is worth passing on is that it won't be what you expect, nor is there a chance for a rehearsal. So if you hear about an idea, and you feel it may be of use, then why not try it?

In this section I give a few ideas. I have outlined the main stages into which labour divides, and said something of what might happen. You will get more information by attending antenatal classes and by reading free booklets given to you by your doctor or midwife. Classes give you the opportunity to understand more of the emotion and excitement, and they let you ask questions, so I recommend them.

The Last Few Weeks of Pregnancy

At the end of your pregnancy you should be having weekly visits to the doctor or midwife. Your baby may be moving about less because there is less room now he is bigger. Also he may have turned. Your doctor will check to see if the baby's head is 'engaged', which means descending into position ready for the birth.

In these last weeks of pregnancy you may feel the muscles of the uterus contracting. The abdomen gets hard and then relaxes. These are not the real thing, just the body having a practice run. These contractions are known as Braxton Hicks' contractions. They are not usually painful.

Towards the end of pregnancy, most mothers-to-be worry whether they will realise when they are going into labour and whether it will all happen too quickly to handle. There are numerous anecdotes about babies being born in the back of the taxi or the hospital car park. My mother's experience was cycling rather rapidly back from the village shop and me popping out an hour or so later! But such examples are the exception rather than the rule. I was not a first child and the birth of a first child generally takes longer.

I think you needn't be too worried about being taken by surprise. For the majority of first births there is usually plenty of time to put a plan into operation. Of course, it is as well to have a plan, and to be aware of questions such as 'what if things start at such and such a time?', 'how will I contact my partner?', 'how long will he take to get home?', 'how will we get to the hospital?', 'is my bag packed?' and so on.

When will things start? Well, there appears to be no good way of knowing. It can be from weeks before your due date until weeks after it. It is not very likely that your baby will appear on precisely the date you have had in your mind for so many months. A first child is more likely to be late rather than early, so try not to get overwrought if your baby doesn't appear on the day he is supposed to. I know it is difficult not to get excited as everything in your life seems to focus on this one date. Perhaps it is worth adjusting your expectation well in advance. I remember feeling a huge sense of anti-climax when Ralph didn't appear on the weekend of the due date. I found the next few days the hardest of all. Where was the baby? Would it ever come? I then thought I should tempt fate by planning all sorts of arrangements including going to an orienteering event on the North Downs and having a curry!

The Onset of Labour

Regular contractions are the most common first sign of the onset of labour. A contraction is a muscular action of the womb as it changes shape to enlarge its opening ready to push out the baby. The womb has a lot to do, but it is by now the largest muscle in your body, so it is perfectly capable of performing its task.

The contractions may start quite mildly and be well spaced out, perhaps one every hour. Labour starts as the contractions get stronger and closer together. Unfortunately there is no universal definition of the start of labour – it is a gradual process which is different for every mother. Advice can vary, but generally you will be told to go into hospital when the contractions have started to come about every ten or fifteen minutes.

Some women will find that their contractions do not follow this 'textbook' pattern, but just start at ten-minute intervals. If this is the case for you, try to judge the strength of the contractions which should gradually increase.

Many women also experience a 'backache' labour, feeling the strength of the contractions more in the lower back, particularly at first, than where they expect, at the front. Again, this is very common and quite usual.

If the pattern of your contractions is not regular, it can be more difficult to decide when to go to the hospital. If you are in doubt, telephone them for advice. A sensible rule of thumb is that you should go in when you are no longer confident that you can cope with the contractions without medical help.

A Show
During pregnancy, the neck of the womb is sealed by a plug of thick mucus. This can come away from the neck of the womb either before labour starts or during the first stage. Called 'a show', it is a small amount of pinkish mucus; pink due to being mixed with a little blood. If you notice a show, you will soon go into labour, but there is no need to rush off to the hospital as it could be another twenty-four hours or so before the stage of your contractions will indicate that the time is ripe. Contact the hospital or midwife if you are not sure. If you have any fresh blood loss you should also contact the hospital.

The Waters Breaking
Your baby has been growing in a sack of fluid which cushions and protects him. That sack breaks during labour – sometimes early, sometimes at second stage. When the waters break, the membranes of this sack give way. This can occur as a gush of water as though someone has pulled the plug out of a basin, or just a constant trickle. The waters can go without any warning. Once the waters have broken, although there may be no other sign of labour, there is a risk of infection entering the womb via the vagina. It is important to contact the hospital immediately.

The Start of my Labour
I was a week overdue when I had the first signs that things were on the move. It started with a show and then some very mild contractions. I felt as though I would be awake all night, as indeed I was. It seems mad now, but I decided to amuse myself by making a fruit cake. It was eventually cooked at three o'clock in the morning. I certainly found it very useful once I came back from hospital.

On the following morning, we rang the hospital and described how I felt and the strength of contractions. The staff were understanding and patiently waited while there were pauses in the conversation as a contraction came and went. I went in and as it seemed not much was likely to happen for some time, went home again (although some hospitals are reluctant to allow you to go home once they have established that labour has started). By midday everything inside seemed more intense and I knew I needed to go into hospital.

Arriving at Hospital

It is useful to discuss either at antenatal class or at a visit to the clinic exactly what will happen to you on arrival at the hospital. In most cases you will be shown to a delivery room where you change into something in which you will feel comfortable for labour. Generally you will need to know your hospital number so that your notes can be found, so have your co-operation card handy. Your temperature, pulse, blood pressure and urine may be checked. You may also have your contractions and the baby's heart beat monitored. This will probably be done by attaching a large strap around your tummy which is connected to a monitor which will 'beep' reassuringly. The midwife will also make an internal examination to see how much the cervix (the neck of the womb) has dilated. That is how wide the opening of the womb now is. The cervix is fully dilated at 10 cm (4 in). You may find that it is only a few centimetres wide at this stage.

Labour

Labour can be divided into three stages. The following is a description of a textbook delivery. Whilst more than 60 per cent of women have no problems, not everyone is like that so I have included a little about some common problems on page 66.

The First Stage

The first stage of labour is when the muscles of the uterus are working to open up the cervix, the neck of the womb. The cervix is fully dilated at 10 cm (4 in). This is a wide enough gap for the baby to come through. This stage, particularly for first-time mothers, may last from around six to twelve hours once the contractions are really under way. For some women, contractions are no more than a discomfort, but for most the stronger contractions at the end of the first stage will become painful.

You may find that controlling your breathing to as relaxed and slow a rhythm as possible will help you cope with the discomfort. A gentle back massage by your partner can also be helpful. There are also various pain relief drugs which you can use (page 65), and when you feel you need help, ask for it. The midwife will not give you any form of pain relief which you do not want, but neither does she want you to suffer unnecessary discomfort. In between contractions, you may feel absolutely fine, and this is the time when your relaxation techniques will come into their own. If you have practised sufficiently, you will be able to relax between contractions so that you are more ready to cope when the next one comes along. By the time you reach the end of first stage, however, you will find that there seems to be little space between the contractions.

Generally you can take up any position you like during labour, except at times of periodic checks by the midwife. Staying upright and moving around will help the muscles to work effectively and keep your labour progressing, so don't just lie on the delivery bed unless you feel that is the most comfortable place for you. Some mothers like to kneel on all fours, others to lean forward against their partner or against a wall while the contraction is at its height.

You will probably be told not to eat anything in case you are sick or in case you need a general anaesthetic. You may be allowed to sip water. If not, moisten your lips with a damp natural sponge or use a little lipsalve if they are dry.

The midwife will monitor the baby's heart rate during this time and check occasionally to see how far the cervix has dilated.

The Second Stage

At the end of first stage, the contractions will be at their strongest, the cervix will be fully dilated and a different set of uterine muscles will take over to push the baby out.

At this transitional stage, you will feel a change in the nature of the contractions, a pressure on the back passage and a desire to push down. Tell the midwife how you are feeling and she will check that the cervix is fully dilated. Some women feel the desire to push for a short time before the cervix is fully dilated and the midwife will need to help them to resist the temptation to push, otherwise the cervix can be damaged. The best way to do this is to try to relax the pelvic floor as much as possible and pant during the height of the contraction. This can also be a very confusing time for your emotions and some women find themselves shouting or trying to get off the bed to go home! You may find it difficult to understand the instructions the midwife is giving you. Try to relax; these feelings quickly pass.

Once the midwife is sure the cervix is fully dilated, you will be able to start working with the uterine contractions to push the baby out through the vagina. This stage can last one to two hours for first-time mothers. At first the urge to push may not be very strong, but as the contractions continue you will not be able to resist it. Remember it is easiest to push if you are squatting, half kneeling or standing, not as is traditional, sitting on your bottom or lying on your back. You may learn different techniques, including concentrating on using the breath to help push the baby out. The midwives will also advise you at the time. Try to feel as though you are pushing from the top of the diaphragm downwards and opening out in the pelvic floor area. If you push too hard in the anal region, you may end up with haemorrhoids.

The top of the baby's head is the first thing to appear and your partner may be the first one to see it. Get him to tell you how things are progressing. Some hospitals have a mirror which they will position at the end of the bed so you can see for yourself how you are getting along. Once the baby's head appears, the midwife will try to help you control the rate at which the head comes through to give the perineum (the area at the back of the vagina) time to stretch and lessen the chance of a tear. She will do this by telling you when to push more gently, and telling you to pant through some contractions in order to allow the uterine muscles alone to do all the work. If it looks as though the perineum will tear awkwardly or won't stretch enough to let the baby's head through, you may need a cut called an episiotomy. This is usually given with a local anaesthetic. At the same time, the midwife will gently ease the baby's head out.

Once the head is out, the midwife checks that the umbilical cord is not round the baby's neck. If it is, it is either slipped over the head or in some cases cut. You will have to push gently to deliver the baby's shoulders, then the rest of the body tends to come out quite easily.

The baby may then be laid on your tummy straight away where any mucus or blood will be wiped away from its nose or mouth or gently sucked away with a soft plastic tube. The cord is cut and clamped (if this hasn't happened already). This will probably happen very close by so you won't lose sight of your new born.

The Third Stage

Once the baby is born, the muscles of the uterus continue to contract in order to push out the placenta, which has now completed its job. In most hospitals, you will be routinely given an injection after second stage to speed up the process. If you are aiming to have an entirely natural birth, assuming everything is normal, and no medical intervention, you may feel you don't want this injection. Do discuss this with your midwife or doctor in advance. This stage is generally not long or painful even though the placenta is a similar size to the baby. The midwife will carefully check the placenta to see that it has come away in one piece. If the baby is late and the placenta has started to break up, parts can be left behind in the womb which can cause problems later. This, however, is unusual.

Once all this is over, you will probably be cleaned up and any tear or episiotomy will be stitched. Your feet will be placed in stirrups for this procedure. The thought of this is not very pleasant, but the reaction of most women, after the rigours of childbirth, is that they just couldn't care.

Depending on the individual hospital, you may be left for a while with your partner and your new baby. Be prepared to feel very emotional and, especially if your labour has been quick, you may feel trembly and shivery. This is all quite usual. You will then be transferred from the delivery suite to the postnatal ward. The length of time you stay will vary from one hospital to another. It may depend on the type of delivery, your health and that of the baby, the availability of spare beds, how busy the labour ward is, and whether a porter is available.

Pain Relief in Labour

When labour starts and you feel any discomfort, there are a number of things you can try to help you relieve the pain. A warm bath or hot water bottle may be soothing or alternatively an ice pack. You can massage yourself, or ask your partner to do this, perhaps rubbing your lower back gently or the shoulders and neck which can get tense. Try relaxation techniques which you may have practised at yoga or antenatal classes, or use the visualisation process described on page 137. Slow steady breathing may also help. Many women also find it helpful to keep moving. Rocking and swaying movements seem particularly effective.

Once you get into hospital you can continue with some of these things. There will also be other forms of pain relief on offer. It is best to find out about these in advance from the midwife or at antenatal classes. You can give some thought as to which you might prefer. Do keep an open mind, though, as no one knows quite how their labour will proceed. You may want to try to have the baby without using any pain relief. For some people that is fine, for others it is not sufficient. Do feel that it is up to you to make the choice and don't be pressured one way or another.

You may be offered gas and oxygen during the first stage or early second stage. You breathe this in through a mask which fits tightly over your mouth and nose or a mouthpiece. Take deep breaths while the contraction is at its height, then stop in between. This relieves the pain and can give a slightly drunken feeling. It has no side effects and does not harm the baby.

TNS is now becoming more popular, but you do need to make arrangements for this while you are pregnant as you may need to take the machine into the hospital with you (see page 56).

Pethidine is the most common drug offered for pain relief during labour. It is given by injection and can cause a variety of reactions from drowsiness, nausea, or a slightly drugged or drunken feeling. Pethidine can pass across the placenta and depress the baby's breathing or make him sleepy. If pethidine is given too near the start of the second stage of your labour, the baby may need an injection to counteract the effect of the pethidine.

An epidural block is a long-acting local anaesthetic administered through a needle in the lower back. It needs to be put in place before your labour is too well advanced, and can be topped up through a fine catheter as labour proceeds. It is usually extremely effective in relieving pain, but does mean that the mother will be immobile with little or no feeling in her legs. She will not be fully able to feel the uterine contractions and will need to be told by the midwife when to push. This makes a forceps delivery more likely.

My Own Labour

My labour was typical in that it certainly didn't turn out as I had expected. Having carefully packed jigsaw puzzles and playing cards to while away the hours of waiting, everything seemed incredibly rushed. After the birth, I realised I was still wearing my socks!

The things I had worried about, such as the pain of the contractions and the episiotomy, didn't seem so bad. It was the unexpected that was harder to cope with. I had wanted to try and do without pain relief and was beginning to cope quite well with contractions using breathing techniques and the TNS machine. Yet suddenly I was violently sick several times, which I found so exhausting that I reached a point of wanting to give in. I opted for pethidine. This worked well for me as it made me feel just one stage removed from everything, even though I knew what was going on. I was able to feel fairly relaxed even when the waters broke and were green instead of clear, indicating the baby was in distress. Perhaps the longest moment of my life, only seconds of course in reality, was the time between Ralph being born and his first cry.

The whole business had its funny moments, too. True to form, even during birth my mind was partly on food. During the second stage of labour, I had some difficulty pushing Ralph out as he was rather big. After some struggling, I said to the assembled delivery team, 'If only we had a smaller loaf, this wouldn't have been a problem.'

Common Problems

Although only a minority of women experience specific difficulties in childbirth, all mums-to-be worry about whether they will be one of the unlucky ones. You may have complications and need special help. The baby may be in an awkward position, or perhaps won't fit through your pelvis. He may not be coping with the stresses of labour which can be shown in the foetal heart rate or the fact that the waters are stained green when they break. You may become too tired to push the baby out.

Many of the problems may require the use of drugs, extra monitoring of the foetus or a specialist or a Caesarean birth. These all help you deliver your baby safely. Some of these problems may be identified before you start labour and, if so, it is reassuring to discuss procedures with the hospital. If you have any other fears or worries about complications it is best to discuss these with your doctor or midwife.

One of the most common procedures is to use forceps to help deliver the baby, and these are used when the doctor feels that the baby needs help to be delivered quickly. Forceps are like large sugar tongs designed so that the ends fit over the baby's head to help to ease it out of the vagina. You will be given an episiotomy if forceps are needed, and may experience more bruising than otherwise. Sometimes, the baby's temples are slightly bruised by the pressure of the forceps, but this soon fades.

Breech Deliveries

If the baby does not turn head downwards by the end of the pregnancy but is positioned with his feet or bottom downwards, it is called a breech presentation. It is possible to deliver vaginally, but you may have to have a Caesarean. You may have an extra scan to check the position of the baby and measure the baby's head. You will then have a pelvic x-ray to measure the size of your pelvic bone. During a normal birth, the baby's head is moulded as it passes down through the pelvic bone. If the bottom is delivered first, this moulding does not take place, so the pelvis needs to be larger than normal in order for the head to pass through. A vaginal delivery may also be inadvisable if you have had other problems during the pregnancy. If this affects you, you should discuss the possibilities with your doctor.

Caesarean Section

The alternative to having a vaginal delivery is a Caesarean section where a cut is made into the uterus from low in the abdomen.

Some women may be told they need a Caesarean because the baby is breech, or the size of the baby's head is too large to fit through their pelvic bone. In the case of these planned Caesareans, you can discuss the details with your doctor or midwife. In other cases, an emergency Caesarean is needed because the baby becomes over-stressed and must be delivered quickly, or the mother becomes too exhausted to push any more. The doctor will make this decision on the spot in the best interests of mother and child.

Caesarean section can be done under general anaesthetic or using an epidural, although if it is an emergency Caesarean it will only be done under epidural if the epidural is already in place and is sufficiently topped up to function properly. The advantage of the epidural is that you are conscious all the time, can see the baby immediately it is born, and do not have to get over the general anaesthetic.

If you have your baby this way it may mean you have to stay in hospital longer to recover. You also need to take care when exercising in order to get your abdominal muscle tone back again.

You and the New Baby

Suddenly the waiting is over and there's a new life in your life. This daunting fact may not strike you in hospital where everything revolves around the baby. There reality, or at least everyday life, could be ignored.

The enormity of the event didn't strike me until I got home some five days later. I suppose it was the return to a place and things not associated before with the birth or with a baby. I remember our first few hours back at home. We sat having a meal chatting about the day; nothing seemed very different. There were just the two of us having a quiet evening. Then came a little murmur from the carry cot on the floor and we realised, 'Yes, that small bundle has come to stay.'

Truth to tell, it really would be easy to recover from the birth if there was some way of the baby disappearing for a few weeks while you got back in shape! Then you could make a proper plan, give him your full attention and get everything sorted out the way you want. Unfortunately it doesn't work like that – there is much more fun. You have to do your best to recover at the same time as looking after him. One major plus point is that the thrill of the miracle of having a baby will help. He is a welcome distraction and starts helping his mummy immediately by insisting he is more important! Maybe you'll sail through. But for expectation's sake it's perhaps best to believe that the going is mostly uphill. However, there are plenty of steps you can take to look after yourself that should help you not only survive but also enjoy your new life as a mum. Your overall diet will help, of course, and I've gone into some detail on this in the next chapter. First though, what sort of state are you likely to be in?

The First Few Days

My mind being totally preoccupied with the baby, it took me about three days to realise I didn't know what I looked like. There seemed to be a shortage of full-length mirrors in the ward I was in. When I finally discovered one in an out-of-the way bathroom, and had a first good look at the 'post-pregnant me' I was horrified! Huge sagging breasts, and worse still, a great jelly bag of a stomach. Wasn't that supposed to have gone once I had given birth? It seems not.

In addition to wondering if your sylph-like shape (because that is definitely how you remember yourself) will ever re-emerge, most women, especially after a first birth, will be quite sore.

The soreness will probably be a mixture. With a straight forward delivery, especially of a first baby, you may well have had some stitches. Forceps deliveries also involve stitches. You may be bruised. You will also be bleeding quite heavily for a few days after the birth. Your breasts will fill with milk and feel anything from fairly hot and swollen to rock hard. You may get sore nipples. You may have piles as a result of all the pushing in the second stage of labour. There is also the possibility of an anal fissure, a tiny tear in the back passage. It may be extremely painful.

This can all sound very depressing, but it probably won't be as bad as it sounds. Something that made me smile was the old theory there's no gain without pain. You end up with the baby and the pain is supposed to make it all worthwhile! After all if it was all like a shopping trip, he might not make such an impact.

Healing

Comfort yourself with the thought that the stitches will probably have healed in ten days to a fortnight. Any bruising will also have lessened by then.

There are several homoeopathic remedies that may help you heal and reduce any bruising. Arnica is excellent. It comes in both tablet and cream form. The tablets are more effective and can be taken in various doses. If you are considering taking these it is worth getting more detailed advice from a homoeopathic doctor. There are some extra large doses that can be prescribed that can be even more effective. Comfrey ointment is another homoeopathic cream which helps bruising particularly. It is very soothing. (Comfrey should not be used on sore nipples as it can be harmful to the baby.)

The essential oil of lavender, used by aromatherapists for its healing and antiseptic qualities, is also worth trying. Put six drops in your bath. The smell itself is very refreshing and cheering. Many people also believe in salting the bath water to help with healing. There isn't any firm evidence to suggest this works, but as my midwife said, if it makes you feel better then do it.

Some hospitals may also provide you with a rubber ring which means you can at least sit comfortably and relax. If these are likely to be in short supply it might be worth buying or borrowing one. Make sure they are strong enough to take your weight. One problem that has recently come to light over the rubber rings is that they may put increased pressure on the thighs and buttocks and perhaps reduce circulation. A comfortable alternative is a very large soft cushion. Ice packs (or a bag of frozen peas well wrapped) can help reduce swelling in much the same way as when they are used on something like a swollen ankle. They are fiddly, though. Take care if you use this idea, as the extreme cold can make the area numb and it is possible to get an ice 'burn'.

Piles or an anal fissure may take longer to heal. A good wholefood diet will really help as it is vital not to be constipated. Look at some of the suggestions outlined in the section below. You may be prescribed an ointment or cream by your doctor. There are homoeopathic creams for both. It is best to get advice from a homoeopath or from a homoeopathic pharmacist. For advice on sore nipples see page 92.

Bleeding

The bleeding that occurs in the few days after the birth isn't usually painful, it is more of a nuisance and a slight discomfort. It helps to have the softest sanitary pads. Old fashioned ones are best. Also have a good method of wearing them. The National Childbirth Trust sell some marvellous inexpensive mesh knickers. They are not the last word in glamour, but are incredibly comfortable and quick to rinse out. The bleeding may be less heavy after three or four days, but expect to have a discharge for some weeks. Change the absorbency of the sanitary pads to suit you.

Constipation

You will be more comfortable in the first few days after the birth if you don't get or even feel constipated. Your choice of food can help with this. Make sure you have a good quantity of fibre-rich foods such as unrefined cereals, wholemeal bread and so on. Be sure to drink plenty of fluids. Dried fruits, especially prunes or prune juice, can also help.

It is very easy to make up a fruit compote by buying a ready mixed bag which usually contains prunes, apricots, peaches and apple rings. Or buy a bag of each type and mix them together in the quantities you like. Boil the fruit until soft in plenty of liquid, then store in the fridge. It will keep for at least a week. Have this with cereal for breakfast in the morning (or as a midnight snack) or serve with yoghurt as a pudding. The compote can be puréed or left whole. If you find soaked dried fruits on their own too rich, chop in some fresh fruit just before eating. As well as helping with constipation, a mixture like this will satisfy a sweet tooth, provide you with iron, and offer natural sugars to give you energy.

Getting Your Figure Back

You may wonder how you will ever get back into pre-pregnancy clothing. Although you may be depressed by your still-expanded waistline, this is not a time to diet as you need plenty of energy to help you recover and cope. Remember if the baby is being breast fed, it is vital that you don't go short of essential nutrients. Crash diets especially should be avoided for this reason. However, eating sensibly should mean that you won't put on extra or unnecessary weight. No, I didn't believe it either until it happened! In the first few months after Ralph was born, I ate enormous quantities of food from breakfast through to late night toast and was amazed to find I didn't put on weight.

Give yourself some time to get your figure back. This may be as much as six months. If, after that time you are still overweight then it may be necessary to diet. By this I mean look at what you are eating and see where the unnecessary calories are coming from. Probably a couple of small changes will make a difference, such as switching to fruit instead of biscuits with mid-morning drinks.

The best way to start to get your figure back initially is to exercise. Your baggy stomach won't disappear overnight but it does diminish noticeably in the first week or so. The midwives will check that your womb is contracting normally. Exercises will help tone your muscles. Apart from your pelvic floor exercise, there are three very simple exercises below to do from day one. Only do as much as you feel able, but aim to increase the number of repetitions gradually. It can feel as though your stitches will burst but it is very rare for that to happen. Apart from starting to tone up your muscles, exercises should speed up the healing process by increasing the circulation. This in turn helps to relieve pain. In addition to the exercises, try to think about your posture. At last that big weight has gone from your front and it can feel wonderful just standing straight. A conscious effort to walk tall will help your muscle tone.

In the chapter on Exercises, there are more details about how to build up a programme for yourself and how to alter it as you get stronger in the months after the birth. Here though are the three simple exercises to begin straight away. (These exercises are repeated in the exercise section.)

Pelvic Tilt

Lie on your back with your knees bent and your feet on the floor. Press the small of your back into the floor using the abdominal muscles, rather like trying to do up the zip on a tight pair of trousers. Hold for a count of four then release. Repeat.

Small Side Bends
Lie flat on the bed with your knees bent and feet flat, your arms by your sides. Reach a little way with the right hand towards the right foot, then return to the straight position and reach with the left hand to the left foot.

Diagonal Reach
Lie flat on the bed with your knees bent and feet flat. Reach with the right hand across the body to the left knee. The head and shoulder only just come off the bed. Breathe out on exertion. Relax and repeat with the opposite arm.

As you recover, you can introduce more exercises and try to fit in a daily walk. It is essential not to do too much too quickly as many of your ligaments, in the lower back particularly, will be soft for several months after the birth.

If you are breast feeding, your abdomen will contract more quickly. Hormones released during breast feeding help the womb contract, which in turn reduces your waistline and abdomen. You may notice a slight twinge a bit like a contraction while you are feeding.

An Emotional Time

What about you? Your physical discomforts may dominate but mentally you are likely to be in a turmoil as well. Elated, relieved, exhausted, amazed, overwhelmed: these are just some of the many emotions you may experience in the first few days.

It can be frustrating being in hospital. It is not the easiest of places to relax. Try to look on the positive side. There are an enormous number of things to do, and to learn. The most important are feeding your baby, changing his nappy, learning to hold him, and bathing him. You can take advantage of all the experienced help there is on hand from the midwives, physiotherapist and obstetricians. The midwives, in particular, have a wealth of experience and a confidence which is inspiring. The food may not be up to much. Look at the suggestions on page 79 on how to make the most of it.

You will probably feel very emotional and weepy, usually in the first days after the birth. Don't be afraid to have a good cry; you will feel better for it.

Some new mothers experience a period of depression a few weeks or even months after the birth. There doesn't seem to be any one cause; the reasons for and the severity of the depression vary from one mother to another. It can be simply a feeling of anti-climax after the birth. It may also be due to the massive hormonal change in the body after birth. About half of new mothers experience some sort of anxiety or depression.

I remember feeling very down-hearted on day three after Ralph was born. It was my birthday and I had been told I could leave hospital, which seemed a lovely birthday present. Half way through the morning, I had a visit from the paediatrician who told me Ralph had lost an unacceptable amount of weight since he was born. We weren't going to be allowed to go home until they were satisfied he was going to put on weight. He queried my breast feeding and suggested that a top up on formula milk would help. This was enough to dissolve me into tears. Not only were we not going home, but I began panicking that something was wrong with Ralph. What confidence I had over my newly learned art of breast feeding took quite a knock.

There was a real team effort from the midwives to try and help Ralph feed. This all coincided with my milk coming through. Sure enough the next day, the little chap had done his stuff and tipped the scales to satisfy the doctor. No need to tape a lead weight to his bottom!

With hindsight I was lucky to have my small crisis of confidence while I was surrounded by so much help and the security of the hospital. Having got over that hurdle, I felt things could only get better.

For some new mothers baby blues can last longer and be more serious. There are things that you can do to help yourself. Talking to friends, family and other new mothers helps put fears and worries into perspective. Trying to get a break from the baby and do something for yourself will give you a boost. If your sense of depression lasts several weeks it is best to get professional advice.

Going Home

The amount of time you spend in hospital will vary greatly. It can be as little as six hours, though generally for new mothers it is likely to be between twenty-four hours and seven days. It is exciting to be setting off home, but also quite a nerve-racking time. Suddenly all the support and professional help on hand in the hospital seems a long way away.

You will get some professional visits, however. Firstly, the midwife may come on a daily basis depending how you and the baby are coping. These visits last until the baby is ten days old. Then the health visitor takes over. Initially she will visit you at home and then arrange appointments for you at the clinic. Here you can weigh your baby, have immunisation, discuss his general development and raise any problems you have.

I looked forward to these visits, finding them most reassuring. I also found them supportive of my desire to breast feed and understanding that I was vegetarian and intending that my child should be. It is important to make your situation clear so that the professionals can give you appropriate advice if necessary.

Apart from professional visitors, it does help if you are able to have company quite frequently in the first few weeks. It may be that your partner is lucky enough to negotiate paternity leave, or you may have other relatives and friends. Don't be tempted to be a hostess. Make sure that your visitors know that part of their job is looking after you. You also need rest and quiet to feed the baby.

Rest

You are likely to be very tired initially with little chance of long periods of sleep. Getting as much rest as you can will help. Rest and a new baby are two concepts that don't exactly go together, but here are a few suggestions.

Firstly, if you are in hospital, you can get a night's sleep. Depending on the time of day (or night) your baby is born, the midwives may offer to take the baby into a nursery to let you get some sleep. Think carefully about this. It may seem dreadful to hand over responsibility so soon, and research shows that baby blues may worsen with such an early parting if for any reason you feel guilty about it. If you are happy about the decision, there is a positive side. Chances are the baby will be asleep most of the first few hours and the sleep you get can be very valuable. If you do decide to let your baby sleep in the nursery, do make it clear that you want to be woken up to breast feed so that the baby isn't started on any sort of bottle – even one that contains water.

Once at home, your baby may sleep or at least nap during the first few weeks. As his day and night clock isn't developed, it may be that he sleeps in the day then keeps you awake at night. Try to see if it's possible to sleep when he does. Don't try and rush round doing all the chores that pile up. They can wait. It is also worth learning to feed your baby whilst lying down (see page 88).

It may seem a paradox but a little exercise will give you more energy. Once you are able, try to get out for a walk every day with your baby. It will help you, and a pram ride or an outing in a sling can sometimes be an easy way to get a baby settled.

The Baby

What should you expect from your baby at this time and what should he expect from you? Rumour has it that new borns just feed and sleep. True, but they sometimes take a great deal of time getting round to both! In between are the nappy changes which, especially if you are breast feeding, are a technicolour experience – usually bright daffodil yellow.

There is no set rule as to how many nappy changes are needed each day, though quite a good pattern to adopt is to change the baby either before or after every feed. Soiled nappies should be changed as soon as possible to prevent the baby getting sore. If you are using terry nappies use the diagram opposite to help you fold them correctly.

Babies' bottoms and faces tend to be the bits that get dirty so make sure these are washed each day using cotton wool and plain warm water. This 'topping and tailing' procedure may be easier than a full bath which many babies don't like. When you do give your baby a bath, make sure you have everything ready – towel, clean nappy and so on. Check the water isn't too hot by testing it with your elbow, not your hand as this can tolerate more heat. Undress your baby and wrap him in a towel. Before putting him in the water, wash his face and hair. Then put him into the bath, holding him by putting one arm under his head and shoulders with your hand holding his body. New borns can be slippery especially if you use soap in the water so get a firm grip. Use your other hand to wash him. If your baby is frightened of water, it can help to have a bath together or use a small container such as a washing up bowl so that the baby's feet touch the sides. This may reassure him.

After the bath, make sure the baby is dried thoroughly in all the creases such as under the armpits and around the neck. In the early days you will also have to pay special attention to the navel. Ask the midwife for advice.

Another aspect of basic baby care is keeping your baby at the right temperature. You should be careful not to get them either too hot or too cold. In hot weather, make sure they are protected from direct sunlight and don't leave them to sleep in a place where they can become overheated. In cold weather, dress them warmly, using layers so that you can take these off once you get somewhere warmer. Hats, bootees and gloves should be used to protect the extremities. The room in which they sleep should be around 65°F (18°C). I found a thermometer most useful to keep a check. Use several layers of bedding as these can be adjusted if the weather is mild. Do be aware that a baby can overheat under a duvet. Babies should not be put to bed in a baby nest for the same reason.

How to Fold a Fabric Nappy (A Kite Fold)

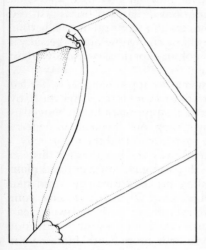

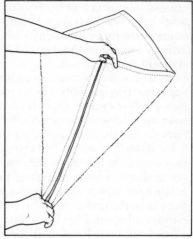

1 Lay the nappy out flat in a diamond shape. Fold one edge into the middle.

2 Fold the second edge in to meet the first edge, forming a kite shape.

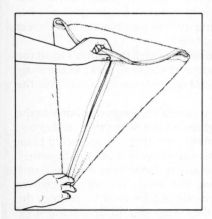

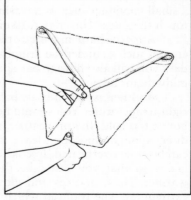

3 Fold the top flap down, making sure that the corners at the top are neat.

4 Fold the bottom point of the kite up to meet the top point.

Apart from keeping your baby fed, clean and warm you also need to keep him entertained. Despite your baby looking somewhat cross-eyed and very floppy, he has already started to take in the world. Very quickly he will get to recognise you, your smell, your voice and also your partner. He will enjoy sounds that you make, singing as well as talking. He'll appreciate strong colours particularly red and green. It is worth putting different cards, pictures of faces or simple items in his cot. Sometimes babies are grizzly for no apparent reason. Check the obvious, such as their nappy, whether they are thirsty and so on. A change of atmosphere or activity can sometimes cheer them up.

Cot Death

Sudden Infant Death Syndrome or Cot Death is a very worrying possibility for many parents. As yet the underlying cause of this syndrome has not been discovered but there are actions you can take to reduce the risk.

- Sleeping: put your baby to sleep on his back (unless your doctor has advised against this for a specific reason).
- Temperature: keep a check on your baby's temperature. Babies can become both cold- and heat-stressed. To check his temperature, don't feel his hands and feet but put your hand on his chest or down the back of his neck as this will give you a more accurate assessment.
- Do not overheat the room where your baby sleeps. It should be between 16 and 20 degrees centigrade.
- Do not use duvets until the baby is old enough to kick them off. Babies should not be put to bed in a baby nest. Cot bumpers should also be avoided as they may restrict the airflow.
- Smoking: try not to smoke during pregnancy. Ideally, give up. Keep the rooms where the baby sleeps and plays smoke-free.

Your Diet After the Birth

It is just as important that you carry on with a good diet after having the baby. In fact, as you can see from what I've described in the previous chapter, you have a great deal to cope with so it is probably even more important. You will need nutritious food to help you recover. Eating good food will also help you cope with the tiredness that is inevitable with a new addition to the family. If you are intending to breast feed, you will need to produce enough milk for your baby which is another demand on your resources.

While You Are in Hospital

Try to get a nutritious diet right from the start. You may be in hospital for several days and have to pick the best you can from the hospital menu. Whilst most hospitals now cater quite well for vegetarians, the choice of meals may not always be brilliant. In my particular hospital there were either variations on dairy food, such as quiche or macaroni cheese, or bean and lentil dishes. I felt I could survive. What I did miss, though, were imaginative salads and crunchy vegetables. Institutional vegetables are very rarely up to much, being well cooked only in the sense of over cooked. It is probably worth having a helping of what is on offer to fill you up and for the sake of variety. It will provide you with useful fibre and there will be some goodness left.

Some things can come as quite a shock. One evening I ordered potatoes and tomatoes with no main course as I needed a change from the beans (and the wind). The standard plate with its un-appealing aluminium cover was put out for me. On lifting the lid, I was confronted with what looked like (and was) the contents of a tin of tomatoes, slightly warmed, swimming round in watery liquid with some plain boiled spuds. Oh for some fresh basil, or even a scattering of chopped parsley. It is all too easy to comfort yourself with some of the stodgy puddings that are invariably part of the menu. Try to stick to the fresh fruit. If the endless oranges and flavourless apples get a bit dull, ask your friends and family to bring in some enticing exotic fruit.

Apart from fruit, it is probably worth thinking of some other foods that you can have brought in fairly easily to improve your diet.

I found a bag of decent muesli invaluable. (Don't forget you'll need a spoon and bowl, too.) Freshly made sandwiches with proper bread and interesting fillings can make a wholesome snack. If you miss your normal variety of salad stuff, a mixture of crudités such as celery, watercress, chopped pepper, cherry tomatoes and so on is easy to transport and not too messy to eat.

When You Go Home

The same good diet principles suggested during and before your pregnancy apply here. You should eat plenty of unrefined carbohydrates such as wholemeal bread, pasta and brown rice; lots of fresh fruit and vegetables; and go easy on high fat products and sugary foods. The main difference now is needing to find the time, energy and inclination to look after yourself. Feeling tired means you won't want to bother with elaborate recipes. Instead you'll need food to fill you which involves minimum preparation. Be prepared, too, for your appetite to change. Many new mothers find that they are absolutely ravenous. My gargantuan appetite lasted all the time I was breast feeding. You'll probably want three good meals each day and still have room for snacks in between. It is a good idea to try to choose nutritious nibbles. A chocolate eclair may seem a treat but it doesn't give your body much to go on.

You may have been sufficiently well organised to fill your freezer and stock up the store cupboard. It is now that you will really appreciate it. Lengthy shopping trips or long sessions in the kitchen are the last thing you'll feel like. If you haven't managed to get quite on top of it, don't worry, there are some short cuts and meals that can be made quite simply.

Breakfast

Don't stint on breakfast as it is an important time to stoke up, especially if you are breast feeding. The body needs plenty of fuel to work on during the day to keep your supplies of milk sufficient. There is a long day ahead and, however good your intentions, there's not always the opportunity to get a proper meal and the time to sit down and enjoy it. You will cope more easily if you are well nourished at the start of the day, and you'll be less likely to feel an eleven o'clock wilt.

Breakfast may be a time when your partner is around to give you a hand which can make it an easier meal still. There are numerous cereals and mueslis which can be boosted nutritionally with extra nuts (choose flaked or ready chopped varieties to save you bother), seeds and dried fruits. Porridge makes a marvellous filling start to the day (not just for winter mothers). Soak the oats the night before to make it quicker to cook, or use the microwave which will save a messy pan. If you like it sweetened, use something like molasses which is rich in iron. If help is on hand, you could also add variety by having something cooked such as mushrooms or beans on toast, scrambled tofu or cooked eggs.

Main Courses

Try to find time to sit down to one proper meal a day. One-pot dishes and casseroles are the easiest things to prepare. Once in the pan they look after themselves and involve very little washing up afterwards. Following this idea doesn't mean sitting down to endless pots of sloppy stew. Depending what you base the dish on, the texture can be varied enormously. A risotto or pilaf from bulgar wheat will be quite different from a more liquid goulash or hot-pot.

Use some sort of grain, pulse or nut to provide the main nutritional content with vegetables and sauce or stock to add colour and variety. Brown rice, buckwheat, millet and bulgar wheat are all very quick to cook. Combinations of grains and pulses are even better nutritionally as they provide you with a good source of protein so save you bothering with an accompaniment. Whole lentils (brown or green) go well with all the grains mentioned, chick peas are good with rice and bulgar wheat, red kidney beans go with rice and buckwheat. Try butter beans with buckwheat.

A combination of grains and nuts give you a well balanced protein. Use almonds, cashews or walnuts for pilafs and risottos. Toast the nuts slightly along with the vegetables before you add the grain, then add the appropriate amount of liquid and cook until the grain is soft.

For goulashes or stews use lentils (red, green or brown) as these don't need soaking; tins of beans or dried chestnuts (soak them for an hour or so before using). Pine kernels and cashew pieces also work well with vegetables in a stew, adding an interesting flavour to the sauce. Either accompany the stew with baked potato, which involves very little work, or a plain pasta or brown rice, both of which are simple to cook.

While you are making an effort, it is just as easy to cook a large quantity to last you several meals, perhaps served in different ways. If you make up a simple lentil hot-pot or aduki bean mix, these can be served under mashed potato, with lasagne or spaghetti, in pastry for pasties, or stuffed into vegetables. Any of these meal ideas on their own would be quite a lot of work, but if your base is already made then they are quick.

Stir-fry meals are also easy to cook. It is no more work than assembling the ingredients for a casserole except everything is cooked immediately and is ready in a few minutes. Stir-fry vegetables on their own are rather lightweight nutritionally so you will need some sort of accompaniment such as rice or noodles. Add extra nutrition to the dish with nuts, seeds, bean sprouts and tofu. If you find chunks of tofu rather bland, use some shoyu or a ready-made French dressing to give it more flavour.

Nut roasts or bakes are fairly easy to put together. You'll need to fry up some vegetables with herbs or spices, add the ground nuts and a bulking ingredient such as breadcrumbs, oatmeal (for a creamy texture) or rice (a more chewy effect), add a little stock and a beaten egg. The advantage of this meal is that anything cold is good as a sandwich filling or a pâté. Nut roasts, having a drier texture, do cry out for a sauce. Why not treat yourself to some ready-made chutneys, pickles or relishes?

Puddings

You may find you have room to eat puddings. Try to make these worthwhile nutritionally, using a variety of fruit and ingredients such as yoghurt. Sweeten them with concentrated fruit juices or honey.

Crumbles are quick to make. Add ground or flaked nuts to ring the changes in the topping. Use mixtures of dried and fresh fruits such as apricot and banana for the filling. Fresh fruit poached and served with yoghurt or crème fraîche is a simple alternative. With a little more effort there are some easy fruit-laden cakes such as carrot and sultana cake in the recipe section which does as a pudding or tea time snack. There are many variations on this recipe.

Fillers, Snacks and Lighter Meals

Grazing is the now fashionable word for eating on the go — very applicable to any new mum. If all the advice about main courses seems too daunting, try some of these suggestions for effortless healthy nibbles. They are not quite three course meals but at least enough to keep you going.

The humble sandwich can have a lot to offer. Buy different breads to give you nutritional variety. Make fillings from any of the following: nut or seed butters, avocado, cheese (cream cheese, goat's, Greek etc.), hummus. Add some fresh ingredients such as watercress, tomatoes, celery, peppers, salad cress, radicchio, lettuce. Finish off with a spoonful of chutney, a dollop of soured cream, French dressing or just lots of black pepper. Serve sandwiches open if you want to pile on more filling and eat them with a knife and fork if you want the sense of having had more than a snack. Try toasted sandwiches for comforting warm food. A sandwich maker is useful, but ordinary grills work well. Why not treat yourself to some special fillings such as cream cheese, celery and apple.

Muesli can make a simple substantial snack any time of day or night. Turn muesli into a meal-in-a-bowl by adding any or all of the following: grated apple, sliced banana, flaked almonds, fruit compote, wheatgerm. Serve the muesli with extra yoghurt, crème fraîche, soya yoghurt or fruit juice.

A baked potato will fill you up and is good value nutritionally. A good sized potato can be microwaved in about six minutes. Wrap it in some kitchen paper towel to keep the moisture in the flesh. Otherwise cook it conventionally. Use conventional fillings such as baked beans (tinned) or grated Cheddar or simply butter and shoyu. For something a little bit different try mixtures of chick pea, olive and tomato; lentil, parsley and spring onion; cottage cheese with herbs and poppy seeds; crumbled Cheshire cheese and walnuts.

Simple soups featuring one ingredient such as carrots, parsnips or celery are easy to cook and provide a comforting base to a meal. Fry up some onion to start with then add herbs or spices, vegetables and finally stock. To make the soup richer, blend with a good knob of butter or with some soured cream. Serving soup with some good bread, rice cakes, pumpernickel or crackers, nut butters and chunks of cheese makes an easy meal.

High-tea style meals such as beans on toast are very satisfying and nutritious as well as being quick and easy.

Normally to get interesting plates of salads, you need to make up several bowls using different ingredients. It can be rather a lot of work. Do a bit of cheating by selecting a number of ingredients such as tomatoes, peppers or celery. Serve them whole or in large chunks. Have a dip on the side instead of mixing in the dressing so what isn't eaten doesn't go soggy. Make a more nutritional platter by serving the salad with bean sprouts or a handful of nuts or seeds, a scattering of sultanas or raisins, cheese, or tofu liberally sprinkled with shoyu or salad dressing.

Bulgar wheat is an invaluable fast salad food. Just soak it in boiling water for a while and then add some well flavoured dressing. It works well with numerous dried fruits, nuts, fresh fruits and vegetables.

You will probably have some cakes and sweets. Whilst these will satisfy your hunger initially, they don't last as long in terms of fuel. You may end up with a long term sweet tooth which could become a weight (and teeth) problem, and these items are mostly high in fat which again won't benefit you in the long term. Try to swap to some more wholesome temptation. Sweet fruit breads, scones and tea cakes, which all tend to be lower in fat and sugar, can just as easily satisfy sweet cravings. 'Heavyweight' cakes such as carrot cake or fruit cake make a better choice if you crave something sweet as these will last longer than insubstantial cream cakes or sweets.

Drinks

As with the later stages of pregnancy, you may still be unusually thirsty, especially if you are breast feeding. Try to stick to water, fruit juices and herbal teas. Ordinary tea and coffee is probably fine with the proviso that they may upset your baby if you are breast feeding. Try to be aware of your need to drink, then drink to quench your thirst. This may be as much as eight cupfuls or glassfuls of liquid a day, but don't force more down than you want as excess fluid can be counter-productive in breast feeding. Try to space your drinks through the day so your body has time to absorb and deal with the fluid. You may need to drink more if the weather is hot. If the urine that either you or your baby produces is very yellow or strong smelling, it could be that you are not drinking enough.

If you are breast feeding it is unwise to drink alcohol as this does go straight into the milk. Having said that, a good slug of brandy (given to the nursing mother) was said to be a foolproof way of getting a baby to sleep. Probably only to be recommended if you get really desperate.

Accepting Help

Whilst this section has been about looking after yourself from a nutritional point of view, bear in mind that during this time you'll probably get lots of offers of help. Anyone who has been a mother will no doubt remember how hard it is at the beginning. You are bound to get floods of visitors, so when they offer help, ask them to bring something edible with them. It may seem cheeky, but they'll be more than happy to oblige and it will give them pleasure when they see the meals being gobbled up.

Breast Feeding

Breast milk is undoubtedly the best food for your baby. It has everything the baby needs to grow strong and healthy. Breast milk contains antibodies that give your baby protection from infections such as coughs, colds and childhood diseases. Breast-fed babies are also less likely to get diarrhoea, constipation or stomach upsets. As your baby grows, the nature of your milk changes so it is always exactly right for your baby.

Once you have mastered the art of breast feeding there are many practical advantages. It is cheap and convenient. You don't have to worry about knowing what is in the milk or how it has been processed. You don't have to bother about bottles and sterilising, nor do you ever need to panic if you get stuck somewhere with no food. It is always on tap, as it were. Another advantage is that breast feeding will help your post-pregnancy tummy go down more quickly. (Though it is true your breasts will remain large for some time.) Above all, breast feeding is an extremely rewarding experience.

Virtually the only disadvantages are possible trouble getting established (in the short term) and the demand it places on you. Mother always has to be around to feed unless you express milk (which then involves you in the business of bottles etc.) which some babies will not take and you must take extra care of yourself to ensure good milk supplies.

Getting Started

Babies know how to suck immediately after birth. This reflex is strongest in the first few hours. It is a good idea to put your baby to your breast as soon as you feel ready. Many mothers do this as soon as the baby is born or within a few hours after the birth. He may suck or simply nuzzle.

For the first three days, you are producing a special milk called colostrum. This has a rich creamy consistency and contains all the nutrients a new born baby needs as well as antibodies to build up the baby's resistance to infections.

Your milk will come in between the second and fifth day after birth. The day this happens can be very uncomfortable as your breasts will feel large and sometimes hot, swollen or hard. This is partly due to the milk but also to extra fluid. The tense, tender feeling doesn't last long, nor will your breasts continue to be so large. You will notice for the first months a 'full' feeling before you feed and an 'empty' one afterwards.

Although your baby may well know how to suck, and you may have plenty to give him, breast feeding isn't necessarily easy at first. Don't assume that you are the only mother who doesn't know how to breast feed your baby – most have had to learn. Do ask (and continue asking) for help from a trusted midwife or skilled helper to help you get going successfully.

The most important thing is to get the baby positioned correctly on the nipple, see illustration below: this is one of the key factors in successful breast feeding. If the baby isn't in the correct position, or you are not comfortable, he cannot feed. Result: sore nipples, hungry and frustrated baby. There may be other problems you will encounter in the first few days. While your milk is coming in, the baby may not be able to latch on properly if your breasts are so full of milk that the nipple is too flat for him to suck on. Result: he cries. Your milk may not come through quickly enough, especially if the baby is large. Result: a day when your baby never seems satisfied, everyone becomes tired and the constant sucking may make you sore.

LATCHING ON

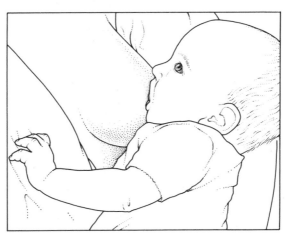

If you have trouble getting going and feel discouraged, think back to the reasons for doing it: it gives your baby the best possible start. Remember, too, that most of the problems ease as you become more confident and experienced.

Do ask for help. Most midwives are very keen to support you if you want to breast feed, and will show you what to do. The NCT also have trained breast feeding counsellors who will be happy to give you advice even if you have not attended their classes.

Learning the Art

To start breast feeding, you need to be comfortable, sitting (see below) or lying down (see page 88), probably propped up with plenty of pillows or cushions. If you are lying down, you may like pillows behind you or under your head.

Breastfeeding: The Sitting Position

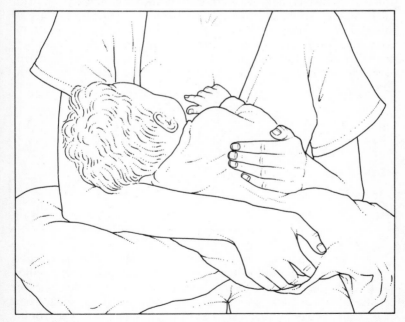

There are several positions you can use and if you get sore it is useful to have a choice. Whether you are sitting (see above) up or lying down, wrap the baby around you, almost like a cummerbund, with his body fully towards yours. Have his mouth just opposite your breast. Make sure you lift the baby towards the breast rather than stretch the breast towards the baby and keep the baby well supported during the feed. The baby needs to get both the nipple and the surrounding area in his mouth if he is going to be able to suck efficiently. There are many pictures of breast feeding babies scarcely on the nipple and having half a loving eye on mum. This is usually a prescription for sore nipples. Don't worry if it looks as though he won't be able to breathe. The nose is a wonderful invention. The little tip keeps the breast away leaving the nostrils clear. Watch for the baby's ears wiggling which shows he is feeding. Check the cheeks don't hollow; if they do it means the baby isn't well latched on.

BREASTFEEDING: LYING DOWN

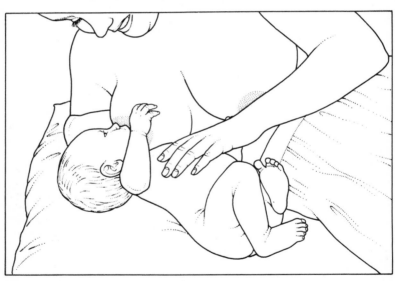

Apart from lying down (see above), or holding the baby across you, you can also hold the baby to one side and lie him on a pillow held under the same arm as the breast on which he is feeding (see illustration on opposite page). As my midwife, who happened to be a man, explained helpfully, just like holding a rugger ball. The trouble is, rugby practice wasn't in my antenatal programme! Nevertheless I found this way of feeding very comfortable. It also made me laugh whenever my husband passed Ralph over for feeding saying 'Do you want the rugby ball'.

BREASTFEEDING: UNDER-ARM

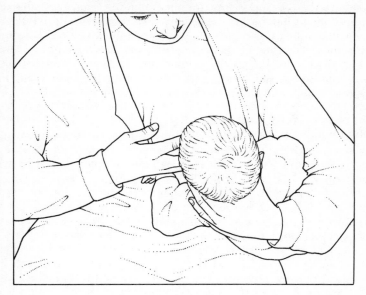

Feeding Times

Most babies feed fairly frequently in the first few weeks, usually every two to four hours. It is amazing how quickly these sessions come round. As time goes on, the feeds may become less frequent.

There was a time when there was no such thing as demand feeding. When I first registered as pregnant I was given a little booklet that stressed the importance of routine, with feeds at six, ten, two, six and ten o'clock. Babies were supposed to settle into a nice neat pattern of feeding every four hours, and no doubt sleep the rest of the time! My husband's grandmother was strictly forbidden to feed at any other times and as a result spent hours pushing the pram round the streets to use up the day.

Thankfully, these notions are now outdated. It may be that your baby does go for four hours, but you may find that it is three, or five, two or sometimes one! It really doesn't matter. If the baby gets his food when he wants it, he will probably be more contented and you'll find if ever you need to stretch the time in between feeds you'll be able to do this more easily.

The time the baby takes on each feed will also vary. Some midwives recommend feeding for ten minutes on each side, others to let the baby feed for as long as he likes. Try not to clock watch but be guided by your baby. You will soon learn to tell if he has fed satisfactorily. If you do take the baby off the breast while he is sucking, never just tug him off. Gently push your little finger between his mouth and your nipple to release the suction first, otherwise the effect will be not dissimilar to a sink plunger on your nipple!

A Diet to Help You

Getting the technicalities right is one thing, of equal importance is having enough milk. Working out how much bottle fed babies need is relatively straightforward. For one day's supply, your baby will need roughly 75 ml (2½ fl oz) milk for every 450 g (1 lb) he weighs. In other words a 3.5 kg (8 lb) baby will need 600 ml (1 pint). For breast fed babies it is much harder to calculate because there is no way to measure how much the baby is drinking. To see if you are giving your baby enough, look for other signs. Your baby should be gaining 150 to 185 g (5 to 7 oz) per week once he has regained his birth weight. There should be periods of the day when he seems satisfied. He shouldn't be floppy but have a good muscle tone and you'll probably be changing about six wet nappies a day. If you feel your supply isn't so good, it is worth trying to put your baby to the breast more often. It is a question of supply and demand. Or rather the more he demands, the more your body should supply.

In addition, your diet will play an important part. Follow all the suggestions on good nutrition already outlined. There is some debate as to whether you need extra calories as well as a good diet, as during this time the body becomes very efficient at metabolising the food taken on board. However, the standard advice is that you may need to consume approximately 500 extra calories per day to help you produce enough milk. It is best to have those extra calories at the start of the day when your system can deal with the intake most efficiently. Follow the suggestions outlined earlier about having a good breakfast.

As the day wears on you will become more tired. This may mean that by the evening slightly less milk is produced. There is no actual proof of this but it is a feeling many mothers have. You can't do much about that except not make the situation any worse. Try not to rush or skip any meals in the day. If you are hungry or feeling low on energy – eat. Just make sure (apart from occasional splurges) that the food you take in is worthwhile – not all sweets and chocolates that will give you calories and little else.

Only a little research has been done into whether some foods are more 'milk-inducing' than others. It is a tradition in some ethnic groups that foods such as aubergines, paw-paw and fresh coconut can help. It certainly doesn't hurt to add these foods to your diet both before and after the birth. Here are a few suggestions on how to use them imaginatively in your diet.

Aubergine pâté is simple to make. Just roast the aubergine in the oven, in the same way as you would bake a potato. It takes about 40 minutes in a hot oven. Scrape out the soft flesh and purée it with lemon juice and oil or tahini. Add garlic and seasonings such as fresh herbs.

Paw-paw is expensive and not to everyone's taste. I think it needs something sharp with it such as lime or lemon juice. Another way to eat it is to purée it with banana and other tropical fruits such as mango.

Fresh coconut can be eaten raw, which is good exercise for your jaw line. It is also pleasant grated into salads or added to curried vegetable mixtures.

Recent research has also shown that malted beers (stout) in moderation promote milk production as they effect the release of prolactin (the hormone that makes milk). Good old-fashioned porridge is also supposed to help milk production as are brewers' yeast tablets (though too many of them may give you a rumbling tummy).

Don't worry about your weight when you are breast feeding. Despite eating more than you may do usually, your figure may return more quickly than if you bottle feed. I found I ate more in the first five or six weeks than I ever had, even when doing long distance running, but I still lost weight.

Equipment

You need very little equipment for breast feeding as the most important items are there already! A good bra is essential for ease of access and to give you good support when you are very full. It is also a good idea if you can start to dress horizontally – in other words something that lifts up at the waist – as this can make breast feeding in public very discreet, much more so than something that buttons down the front.

Breast pads (small shaped absorbent circles) may be necessary depending on the amount of milk you produce. You may leak between feeds or even if you hear your baby (or another) crying. The pads will help protect your clothing. It can be worst in the morning. Finding yourself lying in a wet patch with jets of milk spurting out is not the most pleasant of pictures. Just try and laugh about it.

Breast shells are very useful if you have plenty of milk. It can be the case that when feeding from one side you will drip from the other. The shell just tucks into your bra and will collect the milk, saving a good deal of mess. I sometimes had as much as 25 ml (1 fl oz) collected at each feed. This milk can be stored for a day or frozen for up to three months if you want to have spare milk for emergencies. If you are thinking of doing this the shells need to be sterile.

Breast Feeding Problems

There are some minor discomforts with breast feeding that you might experience, such as feeling swollen or leaking milk. If you are swollen, try expressing a little milk by hand to ease the pressure. Alternatively have a warm bath which will probably mean some milk will flow out. Don't express too much milk, though, or you will make the problem worse as your body will assume that the baby is taking more milk and will therefore produce more. As the baby's feeding pattern becomes established, the problem should ease. If you are leaking, have a good supply of breast pads handy.

Worse problems are sore or cracked nipples which are as bad as you might imagine! It can be a case of grit your teeth every time you feed. Sore nipples are usually the result of the baby not being properly latched on to the breast when feeding. The midwife, health visitor or breast feeding counsellor can help sort that out. Do ask for help rather than suffer and feel that breast feeding should involve pain. Fortunately the body is very quick at healing itself. Between feeds, if you are able, leave yourself exposed to the air. An effective healing ingredient seems to be breast milk itself. After you have fed, rub or pat a few drops of milk on to and around the nipple and let that dry. There are also some very good nipple creams based on ingredients such as chamomile which are very soothing. The advantage with these is that you don't have to wash the cream off in between feeds. Do check that any cream you use contains neither comfrey nor lanolin. Remember, too, that the soreness will persist unless you get the feeding position right.

If you are more than sore and have cracked or bleeding nipples (which I had), nipple shields may help. They are rather like miniature Mexican hats made from latex which you put over the nipple and surrounding area. The disadvantage with them is that they are rather thick and the baby has to suck quite hard to get at the milk. This may lessen the stimulation you get which in turn means your supply goes down. They do give you protection, however, and can be useful as a last resort. I found these very effective for the few days when I was most uncomfortable.

Blocked ducts and mastitis are more serious. The blockage can be caused by missing or rushing a feed, or pressure from restrictive clothing. You may see a red patch on the breast or feel a lump. The first thing to do is to continue feeding, as this should help clear the block. Expressing milk by hand or having a warm bath to get the milk flowing can also help.

Mastitis is an infection which will make you feel achy as though you are getting 'flu. You should see the doctor as soon as possible who will provide antibiotics. These don't prevent you from feeding, but be aware that the baby may get diarrhoea.

Finally, if your positioning is good and you still feel very sore it could be a case of candida or thrush. Talk this over with your doctor or health visitor as there are various remedies.

I hope outlining these problems doesn't put you off. There are bound to be times when you feel a little low, but it will soon pass. The good that you are doing your baby will last so much longer. Some mothers do get a great feeling from breast feeding and are very reluctant to stop. I was never a particularly passionate breast feeder but after about a month I felt a wonderful sense of ease. It all became part of the routine and I started making telephone calls or reading while I was feeding. I was glad I had stuck at it and succeeded.

Bottle Feeding

It is estimated that 98 per cent of women are capable of successful breast feeding. For a few it is not possible. This could be due to a hormonal imbalance or because they are on certain medications. Women with flat or inverted nipples may have a problem, too, but they can still breast feed if they wish; ask your midwife or NCT breastfeeding counsellor for advice. If you can't breast feed for any reason you will need to find an infant formula milk for bottle feeding. There are now several on the market that are vegetarian. Some brands state this on the packet or bottle. Otherwise check the ingredients carefully. Beef fat or other animal fats are usually what makes the product non-vegetarian.

There is one formula milk based on soya milk that is vegan (some others are advertised as such but are, in fact, not acceptable). Ask in your local health food shop. If you have any doubts get in touch with the Vegan Society (see page 169). You may find non-dairy formula milk useful if your baby has lactose intolerance or is allergic to cows' milk products.

Bottle Feeding Equipment

There are numerous types of bottles and teats available. It is probably worth asking your midwife, health visitor, doctor or NCT group for advice on the pros and cons of the various models. You will need six bottles and teats so that you are always sure to have a couple ready cleaned and sterilised. You will also need some way of sterilising your equipment, either a specially designed unit or a large saucepan. A bottle brush is handy for cleaning the bottles and the teats. The most important point to remember when using bottles is to keep up a good standard of hygiene and not just for the first few weeks. Many babies get gastroenteritis after three months, when parents get a little slack. You might consider buying a steam steriliser which is quick to use but quite expensive.

Ready-made formula milks are available in cartons. Sometimes your baby may not like the taste of these as they are thicker and more strongly flavoured than the powdered milk.

Colic

One of the hardest things to come to terms with with your new born is colic. No one quite knows why babies get it or exactly what it is. Colic is thought to be caused by foods in the stomach almost fermenting, then causing pain and wind as they pass down the gut. What you see is a very fretful baby, screaming in agony, often bright red in the face with a tense, rigid body. An attack may last on and off for a whole evening. Colic can start any time from the first week to ten days and last up to three months. At one time it was thought that breast-fed babies are supposed to be less susceptible but this appears to be a myth.

There is very little you can do except try to relax. This is more difficult than it sounds as you are convinced that there is something dreadfully wrong and can feel helpless. Obviously check with your GP if there is any doubt in your mind. Doctors are very understanding about parental anxieties. Then make sure there is no simple cause. Is the baby hungry, too hot, too cold, uncomfortable, wet or dirty?

If it is colic, it can help to cuddle your baby very tightly, and use rhythmic rocking motions, either sitting down or walking round the room. Some babies are soothed by being put on your lap, face down, so their tummy is across your knees. Then gently rub their back. Another position that can be helpful is to hold the baby face up. Gently bring each of his legs up across his stomach, bending at the knee. Do this one leg at a time. This is similar to a yoga position that is supposed to relieve wind. A warm hot-water bottle, well wrapped, on the tummy may also help. Taking the baby's nappy off is also worth trying.

Herbal teas made with boiling water and left to cool can be tried. Chamomile and fennel are thought to be effective. Only give two to three teaspoonfuls on a sterilised spoon. You may also be able to soothe your baby by feeding at the breast. The old-fashioned (and still popular) remedy was gripe water. The main drawback is that most brands have either sugar or alcohol added. Get advice from your health visitor or doctor before trying these.

Something less traditional, in fact controversial, is cranial osteopathy. This technique works on the theory that the baby's head is moulded and squashed during birth. This may distort the base of the cranium where there are important nerves including those that affect digestion. The osteopath uses very gentle pressure from his hands to ease this area. Success can vary, though many doctors dismiss the practice. However, if hours of screaming make you desperate, alternatives are often worth a try. Parents I spoke to had been very impressed. For more information get in touch with a registered osteopath.

First Foods

It is not difficult to prepare all the solid food your baby will need in your own kitchen. I hope this chapter will give you information to be able to do that, regardless of whether you choose a vegetarian diet or not. The chapter is arranged with some general comments before four sections discussing aspects of baby food for particular ages.

Deciding when to start solids, what to give and how to go about it can be daunting. If you have been exclusively breast feeding, introducing food from the outside world may seem akin to letting aliens intrude on your baby! First foods are rather like their first steps into the world without you; no sooner does the first teaspoonful of apple purée pass their lips than you can see the little treasure toddling off to school with a packed lunch of bean pasties and peanut butter sandwiches.

First things first. There is no rush. All a baby needs for the first few months, probably at least four and in some cases six, is milk. Even after six months he can still get the majority of his calories and nutrients from milk, either yours or formula. Virtually the only nutrient there can be a problem about is iron. The baby should have enough to last him for the first six months, from then on he needs iron from an outside source. I do know there are arguments for the rapid introduction of solids. Apart from whatever you feel and your initial wishes, you will feel pressure to give junior solid food within weeks rather than months. It may worry you! Those who haven't had babies are often amazed that someone can still be breast feeding six weeks after the birth, let alone six months later. And manufacturers label a wide range of food as being suitable from three months, which adds to the feeling that babies need something else other than milk by then.

I take the view that it is best to leave introducing solids until your baby is really ready for them. There are several reasons for this: it allows the digestive system to become more mature, it reduces the risk of adverse allergic reactions, it checks any tendency to over-feeding, and it is practical, in the sense that milk is easier than solids to have ready! I will say a little more about each of these points.

Babies have immature digestive systems when they are born. It takes about three months for their stomachs and intestines to cope comfortably with anything other than milk. From then on different foods can be introduced gradually.

Introducing certain foods too early, such as wheat or dairy products, might increase the likelihood of an allergic reaction. Some babies do react to substances that are in certain foods, and generally speaking they may not do so, or may do so less violently, once they are a little bit older.

It is also possible that starting solids too early may lead to overfeeding. If the baby has a full quota of milk and on top of that food he doesn't really need, he may take up unnecessary calories. In turn these can turn to extra fat. There is the possibility that this could start a long-term weight problem. More short-term it may mean he is slower to sit up, crawl, stand and walk.

There is the purely practical point, too. Once you introduce food there is a lot of extra work cooking and clearing up. Don't forget how clean and convenient breast feeding is or how well organised you are with your bottle feeding routine. It is much easier to travel with your baby when breast feeding compared to when he is on solid foods.

The only disadvantage, it seems, of leaving introducing food too late, is that your baby may feel that milk is the only food to eat! He could be unreceptive to anything else, making it harder to get the concept of eating established. Bearing the above in mind, if you are happy with the way you are feeding, and producing a sufficient supply of milk, and if your baby is content then there is no need to start on solids.

When Should You Start?

There are several signs which show that a change is needed. The three main ones are the baby's weight, the baby's physical development, and the number of feeds required per day.

The weight of the baby is a good indication because the more he weighs the more food he needs. Once he weighs about 6.5 kg (14 lb) or more, a baby needs over 900 ml (1½ pints) of milk per day to keep up his energy and growth. This is not only a lot for you to produce, it's also an enormous amount for him to drink. His stomach may be full before he has drunk enough, so he will reduce the time between feeds. At about this weight, a small amount of solid foods adds just a few extra calories but doesn't extend the stomach too much.

Another sign of a need for solid food is the number of feeds the baby requires. He becomes less content with the established number. You may suddenly find that whereas he has been having five or six feeds a day and a long sleep during the night, your baby demands more frequent feeds, wakes in the night and doesn't ever seem quite satisfied.

A further indication for solid food is the baby's physical development. Around three to four months your baby will reach a new stage. Having learnt a basic grab, he will start to put everything he is offered straight to his mouth. This is one of his main ways of exploring the world. Obviously this is a very useful stage at which to be when introducing food.

Even with all these clear signs, you may still want to delay starting on solids. From a purely selfish point of view it needs to be a good time for you. Just think through the next few weeks. If you are about to be away on holiday, for example, then perhaps wait to start until you are at home. You then don't have to worry about extra equipment while you are away.

Looking back on the diary I kept after Ralph was born, I note I had set a target in my mind that I wanted to breast feed until at least four months. After that I would then see how it went from week to week. As the first few months went by I thought it was going so well that I would go on until five or six months. Things didn't quite work out like that, however. At just over three months Ralph got two sharp bottom teeth. A few days later he began a phase of waking in the night. He had been a good sleeper from five weeks. Now, at two or three in the morning, there would be enough loud yelling to wake me up. When I picked him out of his cot, he would suck my cheek vigorously as though desperately hungry. At this time, he weighed about 6.75 kg (15 lb). So after our return from a Christmas break, I decided to start him on solids just a day or so before he reached four months.

Starting with Solids

Whatever you decide, every baby will take to solids differently. If you are starting too early your baby may reject everything on offer. Don't panic. Just leave the whole idea for three or four days and start again. Initially you are offering food only as a supplement and your baby won't suffer if he goes without this. Some babies will be slower to get used to foods, others may display a large appetite fairly soon. They'll soon tell you if they are not happy.

Other factors may alter their desire to feed. Commonly teething, illness or a change in routine will do this. Be patient. It will take you several weeks to build up to any sort of sizeable meals, and up to a year or more before junior will be tucking into meals with the family.

Out of interest, I kept a record of Ralph's progress towards solids. Overall I remember it as a gentle process. Starting with no more than half a teaspoon, it took roughly three weeks to get to two very tiny meals of three to four teaspoonfuls. He would have the same mild flavour for three days at a time. It was a further three weeks of building up to what I remember feeling was 'serious' food. This was three meals. Breakfast was a tablespoon of baby rice. A midday meal was half of a banana puréed with a couple of prunes and a piece of melon. His supper was a puréed carrot with a little parsnip. By that time I had dropped down to either three or four milk feeds a day. (I found there was inevitable variation from day to day.)

Just after he turned six months, Ralph's interest in food seemed to overtake his desire to suck. In the morning he was very happy to be offered cereal first rather than the breast. About this time, he also began to accept a slightly coarser texture rather than purée which meant I could introduce a baby version of muesli.

By seven months I was down to two milk feeds a day and he was keen on finger foods such as chunks of pear, rice cakes and bread. I wasn't always so keen on these as I watched huge chunks disappearing down his throat. Usually they reappeared, but I always hovered just by ready to turn him upside down. Luckily this was never necessary.

As the quantity in the meals built up Ralph began drinking more water and very diluted juice made from concentrated apple juice. At around seven months I started him on very small quantities of organic cows' milk. Once it seemed as though he suffered no reaction, he began drinking about 300 ml ($^{1}/_{2}$ pint) a day.

I stopped breast feeding at around eight months. By this time I had stopped measuring his food in tablespoons as he seemed to need a bowlful at each meal supplemented by fresh fruit, yoghurt puddings and bread or toast. Although the range of food I had introduced was now much wider, the mixtures still tended to be quite well mashed or even puréed. At around eleven months Ralph was prepared to eat much coarser textures which soon made it possible for him to eat small portions of our meals as long as they were suitable. He could also cope with sandwiches which made picnicking much easier. At around a year he would hold a spoon and work his way through about half a bowlful before getting bored and deciding to play with the rest with his hands.

To help you introduce your baby to solid foods I have outlined four different stages. The first stage may start between four and six months and concentrates on what sort of foods you can try and how to help your baby to learn the idea of eating. The second stage is after six months when the range of food you can introduce broadens. The third stage explains how to make the transition from breast feeding. Finally the fourth stage looks at what sort of food you might expect your baby to eat once he's a year or so old and how to encourage healthy eating through todddlerhood.

Hygiene

It is vital to be hygienic when you prepare your baby's food and drink. Sick babies are more tiring and less fun. Wash your hands before preparing any food. If you have finger nails of any length make sure they are well scrubbed. Wash knives, boards and items such as a sieve or processor thoroughly each time they are used. Rinse them well in hot water. Utensils such as the baby's plate and spoon should be sterilised by being boiled thoroughly before the first use. Then always wash them well in hot soapy water, and rinse in boiling water. Dry only with a clean tea towel. Anything washed in a dishwasher will not need to be rinsed or dried and should be sterile.

If your baby doesn't eat all you've prepared, throw it away. It is very little wastage. If you are serving larger quantities and you are not sure how much he will eat, put half the mixture only in a bowl. Add more when he has finished. Only save food that has not been in contact with the spoon he has used.

If you are preparing large batches of food to refrigerate or freeze, try to cool the mixtures quickly. Portion into containers and put in the fridge or freezer as soon as possible. A good way to freeze food for tiny stomachs is in ice cube trays. Sterilise these by boiling well then fill with a food mixture. Defrost as needed.

Any water you give your baby for drinking should be boiled and then cooled.

Stage 1: from about Four Months

The following section looks at how you should introduce solids with suggestions as to which foods you might try and how to prepare them. With anything you try, be prepared to be flexible and watch your baby's reaction to the food. It may be spat out immediately. Don't worry, this isn't always a sign of dislike. Sometimes it may just be that the taste is a little strong or the texture isn't to his liking. It is worth trying that same food again several days later. On the other hand, the food may be eaten with relish and then your baby finds out it doesn't like him. Ralph seemed to enjoy puréed apple, eating three or four teaspoonfuls at his first attempt, only to have dreadful stomach ache later.

First Foods to Try

Cereals used to be the traditional first foods. These were readily available and cheap, as well as being a nutritious and staple part of the diet. Their bland flavours appealed to the infant taste buds. Cereals could easily be made into gruels and runny porridge without the use of modern gadgets that we take for granted. Now, because of their wide availability, many fruits and vegetables are also thought suitable for first foods.

Cereals

There is no reason not to stick with tradition and try cereals. Rice is now considered the best cereal on which to start your baby as it is a very easy grain to digest. It also contains no gluten, a substance found principally in wheat and to which some babies are allergic. Their digestion lacks the ability to cope with it, and the body reacts to it. The reaction can cause a condition known as coeliac disease. Cereals containing gluten are probably best left until a little later. Initially you can buy special 'baby rice', a dry powder or flaked product. The main advantage of these is that the powder form means you can mix exactly what you want very easily. As you may only want a teaspoon or less, it is really not worth going to the trouble of cooking and mashing anything yourself. You can make up the baby rice by mixing the powder with either boiled water, breast milk or formula milk. Some of the baby rice mixtures contain small amounts of soya flour and maize meal, both of which are gluten free. When mixed up, this recipe has a golden colour rather like polenta and a very slightly different flavour. Your baby may prefer one mixture to another.

Special baby cereals are usually fortified with a vitamin and mineral mixture. This is probably not strictly necessary but is more of a vitamin insurance policy. It can add to your confidence that the baby will get nutrients as the supply of milk from you reduces.

Once your baby starts to eat larger quantities, then you can give larger portions of baby rice. Use up to two tablespoons of powder. If you don't want to buy any commercial products, you can bulk cook ordinary rice and freeze it in usable portions. By ordinary rice, I mean white rice, as at this stage the fibre in brown rice can be too much for your baby's delicate system.

How to Prepare Cereals

Mix baby rice according to instructions using a little cooled boiled water, breast milk or ready mixed formula milk. When mixing just a small quantity, such as two teaspoons, it is easy to mix the liquid into the powder. Once your baby will eat a larger amount, such as two tablespoons, then do it the other way round to avoid lumps. Measure the required amount of the liquid into the bowl first, then sprinkle the powder over the top and mix in gradually.

To make your own baby rice, measure out a portion of rice in a cup or jug and put it into a saucepan. Then add four times the volume of water. Bring to the boil and simmer, covered, until very soft. This may take as long as 40 minutes. Drain if necessary. The liquid can be saved for mixing with cooked vegetables. Mash, sieve or blend the rice until completely smooth.

Fruit and Vegetables
Fruit or vegetable purées can also be introduced as first foods. Again, bear in mind that you will only need tiny quantities. A banana or pear is easy as it's simply a matter of mashing up a small piece. Using these purées (instead of or to alternate with rice if you wish) gives your baby a chance to try different flavours. Don't worry if at this stage he only likes a very limited range. After all his diet for the past four months or so has been confined to just one taste, milk.

Advice as to which fruit or vegetable to choose is quite varied. In general terms it is best to go for fruit and vegetables that are not too strongly flavoured and not too fibrous. The most popular of these are apples, pears, apricots, carrot, parsnip and sweet potato. You can also try avocado pear (for babies with expensive tastes).

It is best to leave the brassicas such as cabbage until feeding is well established, say after two to three months. Even adults suffer from trying to digest these, so your baby may have the same problem. Broccoli and cauliflower may not be liked by your baby at first. Spinach, too, is best avoided. It is not only strongly flavoured, but also contains high levels of oxalic acid. This is thought to limit absorption of calcium in food that is eaten at the same time.

The citrus fruits can cause reactions and are best avoided for the first few months of feeding. Paradoxically you can give very diluted orange juice (one part orange to four parts water).

How to Prepare Fruits and Vegetables
- Apples: choose a dessert variety. Peel, core and chop then cook in a little water until soft. Mash very well with a fork, sieve or blend.
- Apricots: use a dried variety. Wash them well, looking especially for little pieces of grit that sometimes get caught in the folds of the fruit. Soak for at least two hours or overnight. Cook for 40 minutes or until fairly soft. Sieve or blend

until smooth. Other dried fruits such as prunes, peaches and pears can be prepared in the same way.

- Avocado: peel and mash or blend a small quantity. Remember that avocado has a high saturated fat content, so even if your baby likes it, don't use it for too many meals.
- Banana: choose a ripe fruit. Peel, remove the stringy pieces on the outside and mash very well, sieve or blend. The little seeds in the centre will show in your baby's nappy as tiny red-gold threads. Don't panic!
- Melon: choose sweet ripe varieties such as Galia or Chantilly. Carefully remove all the seeds, then mash, sieve or blend.
- Pears: choose ripe sweet varieties such as William or Packham. Peel, core and chop. If very ripe, mash without cooking. Otherwise cook until just soft in a little water. Then mash, sieve or blend.
- Carrots, potatoes, parsnips, sweet potato, courgettes: peel and trim the vegetables first. Initially all vegetables should be given cooked. Do this by steaming, microwaving or boiling in a minimum amount of water to preserve as many of the nutrients as possible. When soft, drain and mash well, sieve or blend.

Texture and Consistency
Up to now all your baby has had is milk to drink; he hasn't learnt how to cope with much in the way of texture. First foods therefore need to be very sloppy. Any purée you make should be quite thin with the consistency of double cream. If you are making up too small a quantity to work in a blender, push the food through a fine sieve. For a couple of teaspoons this isn't much effort. If your baby appears to gag on a new food, it may be that the texture of the purée is too difficult for him to manage.

Temperature
Although the milk he drinks from you or the bottle is warm, you don't necessarily have to feed the baby warm food. You might find it less trouble to serve food at room temperature. It does make life easier when you go out for the day, for example, as you don't have any worry about heating up food. Food certainly should never be hot. Babies cannot tolerate the same amount of heat in food as well as we can. Alternatively meals shouldn't be served straight from the fridge as this would be too cold. Be very careful if you use a microwave to defrost portions of frozen food, or even to take the chill off

foods from the fridge. Hot spots may well develop in the mixture because of the way the microwave cooks. Stir any food well both during the re-heating process and afterwards. Then let it stand for a few minutes to be sure.

Equipment
You don't need to have any special equipment to prepare baby food. Electric gadgets such as a blender or food processor are quicker and less effort than using a fork to mash or pushing ingredients through a sieve, but the result is the same. For very small quantities you can buy little hand graters which work very well, reducing soft food to a pulp. Do follow the advice on hygiene.

There are special food warmers you can buy which work for both food and drink. These are filled with water and the food is then heated in a container in the hot water. Using a timer means you can check the food doesn't get too hot. Careful use of a microwave or improvisation by using a bowl in a pan of hot water will also work.

How to Introduce Solids
Once you have decided your baby is ready for food, it is then a matter of experimenting to find out what he likes and what he doesn't like. The aim is to get the baby eventually to enjoy a sufficiently wide range of foods so that when he is about a year old he can eat what you eat. Another aim is to establish healthy eating patterns right from the start. First, though, you also have to introduce him to the whole concept of eating, which can be quite a lot of fun, games and mess.

Start introducing food at one of your daytime feeds. The morning is generally not the best time. Then, the baby is usually at his hungriest and ready to suck at the familiar breast or bottle. Midday or early afternoon seems to work well. This also has the advantage of allowing you plenty of time to see if the food is causing any ill effects during the rest of the day rather than have the baby up all night with an upset tummy.

Initially you need very tiny quantities, say half to two teaspoonfuls. This is really just a taster to check for an adverse reaction. If you are breast feeding, feed on one side as usual. If bottle feeding, stop roughly half way through. Then, whilst holding your baby in your arms, put a tiny amount of food on the tip of a little spoon and let the baby suck it off. Don't worry if most of it simply dribbles back out. It may take two or three goes for him to understand that he is supposed to swallow the stuff.

For the first month to six weeks, be careful how you introduce each food. Prepare it on its own and then try it for three days just to check there are no ill effects. On the first try, don't be guided entirely by the baby. He may well decide to gobble down several spoonfuls only to find later it doesn't like him. On the second day, if all is well, you can give him a little more.

Build up a range of 'safe' foods gradually. Once he has got the idea of eating and you are happy about his reaction to the food, then you can increase the quantities. At this stage, your baby will probably show you when he has had enough. One day a single table-spoonful may satisfy, the next day he may go for two or three times as much. It is a good idea to offer drinks of plain water along with the meal. During this stage your baby may or may not give up one breast or bottle feed.

At first, keep all these meals very simple, just one food at a time. This makes it easier for the baby's digestive system to cope. Once feeding has increased to two or three meals a day, each of two or three tablespoons, it is well established, and then mixed meals can be started. Example combinations are baby rice and carrot purée, apricot and banana purée.

Be prepared for nappy contents to change in texture and sadly to smell, too. Gone are the days of the almost sweet smelling daffodil colour motions. Different food will come out quite differently. Lots of avocado will make the stuff green, small red threads will be evident with first mouthfuls of banana. You may also find that even with as little as a teaspoon of solid food, the baby may not pass motions so frequently. This is usually nothing to worry about as long as the baby is happy. If he starts to strain excessively, actually to the point of crying, when passing a stool, he is likely to be constipated.

The classic remedy is a sugar solution which has the effect of drawing more liquid into the gut, thus making the motions softer and easier to pass. Bang go the healthy eating ideas! You may have to resort to this. First, though, make sure your baby is getting plenty to drink. Offer it if necessary at every opportunity. Cooled plain boiled water is fine, or very diluted fruit juice (one teaspoonful in six to eight teaspoons of water). If you are using a concentrated juice, try one teaspoonful in 250 ml (8 fl oz) of water. Another remedy for constipation is a prune purée. It is naturally sweet so the baby should enjoy it and it has laxative qualities that should help.

Foods to Avoid

Even at this stage, babies will have quite varied diets influenced by their own mother's likes, what is in season and of course what they will eat. There are some foods that should be avoided for the safety of your child. Some rules apply long term, some just up to six months.

For the first 6 months do not give your baby cows' milk or any milk products such as yoghurt, cheese or butter. This is because the baby can develop an allergy to these products if introduced too early.

Do not introduce foods containing gluten such as bread and pasta. Generally gluten is associated with wheat products.

Do not give any eggs (yolks or white) as these, too, can cause allergies.

Do not add any salt or sugar to your baby's food. They do not need it. Their immature kidneys cannot cope with salt.

Small hard pieces of food such as pieces of nuts are easy to choke on. Avoid these until the child can chew really well (at least two years old). Ground nuts are fine before this. Peanuts are also dangerous in that if inhaled they can release toxins into the lungs.

Stage 2: from about Six Months

The baby's sixth month marks a watershed in feeding. Up to this time, he is probably still having a high proportion of breast milk or formula milk. Those first tastes of solids do give him some satisfaction, but it is almost more important in the first stage that he gets the general idea of eating rather than that you worry about the general balance of his diet. From around six to eight months this becomes something to consider. It is both useful and important to extend the range of things he can and will eat, as he relies more and more on solid food for his nutrients.

Foods to Try and How to Prepare Them

Your baby needs to be able to eat a range of staple foods from the groups that you use as adults. These are the grains, nuts and seeds, pulses and dairy products. For a baby, though, you can't always prepare these foods using the same recipes as you would for an adult. A six month old isn't going to tuck into chilli and rice (although it is amazing how many babies really like hummus, including the garlic!). He might eat a simple lentil bake and mashed brown rice, however.

Judging whether your baby is ready for a more demanding food has to be an individual decision. If your baby eats it and has no obvious stomach ache and no sore bottom after passing a motion, he can probably cope. Bearing this in mind, try introducing the foods listed below between six to eight months and a year. I'll start by describing the cereals.

Millet

Millet is a marvellous cereal to introduce to babies. It is rich in the vitamin B group as well as containing good levels of iron and amino acids which make up proteins. It has a pleasant mild flavour that goes well with both vegetable and fruit dishes. It is easy and quick to cook and very rarely contains any indigestible husks that sometimes crop up in barley or wheat. You are unlikely to find millet in supermarkets so it needs searching out in health food shops.

To cook it, use a small cup to measure the grains and cook in three times as much water. Bring to the boil and simmer, covered, for 25 minutes or until soft. Add extra water if necessary. Initially mash the millet well, blend or press through a sieve. As your baby learns to cope with coarser mixtures you need only break down the grains slightly.

Millet flakes are also available. These take only minutes to cook. Use about one part millet flakes to two parts water.

Oats

Oats cook to a creamy grain. They can be made into porridge, but can also be used to thicken burger mixtures and vegetable bakes. Oats are rich in the vitamin B group as well as being a good source of protein.

Baby porridge is rather like adult porridge to cook, using one part oats to two and a half parts water. Once cooked, you may like to thin the mixture down with milk or soya milk. Do not add salt. Sweeten with concentrated apple juice, malt extract or honey.

Rice

If you haven't already started your baby on brown rice you can try some now. It is a grain that is rich in the vitamin B group and amino acids. As with millet, be sure to cook the rice well and sieve or mash to a texture your baby will enjoy.

Cook brown rice in three times as much water until really soft. Then mash it well.

Apart from cooking brown rice there are various rice products you can buy that make useful snacks and quick meals. Rice cakes are made from puffed rice. These are a good alternative to rusks and biscuits, many of which have added sugar. Adults can find them bland, but babies enjoy them. Some varieties of rice cake are slightly salted but there are plain versions, as well as mixed grain or some with added sesame seeds. At first giving one of these cakes can be a little nerve-racking when the whole thing breaks apart in the baby's mouth. Stand ready to do some back slapping and fishing out. Most of the larger pieces just fall out. Often the baby will suck on the cake until it goes soggy and is then easy to swallow. You can spread the cakes with a little yeast extract, smooth nut butter or sugar-free fruit spreads. Be prepared to fend off comments such as 'what are you giving him, a polystyrene ceiling tile!'

Plain puffed rice is also on sale in health food shops. This makes a good breakfast cereal and can be mixed with fruit or vegetables to make more nutritious main courses.

Muesli
There are several versions of baby muesli and breakfast cereals on the market. Sadly very few of these are sugar-free, having either ordinary sugar or glucose, dextrose or maltose added. I found a Swiss make that contained oat, wheat and rye flakes, shredded dates, apple and banana, ground almonds and wheatgerm. This can be served with water, fruit juice, milk or diluted soya milk.

Making your own muesli is easy, especially in large quantities which can be ground in the food processor. It will store well.

Baby Muesli
4 parts oats
2 parts millet flakes
1 part mixed flakes (muesli base)
2 parts chopped dates
1 part ground almonds
1 part wheatgerm

Mix all the ingredients and blend until reduced to a coarse powder. Serve with milk, soya milk or water.

You can vary the ingredients I've suggested to suit your own child.

Wheat
Wheat products are not given to babies of less than six months old because of a possible gluten allergy. If there is any history of this in your own family then it is best to leave wheat (including bread and pasta) until the baby is over a year old. The allergy may still surface then but it is easier to diagnose and treat.

If you are able to introduce wheat, some time around the seven to eight month mark, you can give mashed cooked pasta and bread. The timing depends on your baby's ability to manage the rougher texture of these foods. Depending on your baby's ability to chew (and your confidence) you can give a whole crust. This can occupy him for several minutes while he does a combination of sucking and chewing. Alternatively, cut the bread into small infant bite-sized pieces and let him feed himself. Don't be too despondent if the first time he sees the neat little squares cut up and ready, he picks up the plate and chews that instead! He'll soon find out which bit is more edible. Eating bread is a step nearer to sandwiches, useful as a meal if you are out for the day. On the bread, you can try a variety of nutritious spreads such as smooth nut butters, a scraping of yeast extract or a fruit spread.

Fruit and Vegetables

Your baby will now be able to eat more fibrous vegetables such as leeks as well as those with a more definite flavour such as tomatoes, broccoli and mushrooms. You needn't necessarily introduce these new items on their own as you did with the first phase of feeding. Mix them with other vegetables you know to be 'safe'. If your baby shows any adverse reaction, drop them out of the diet for a while.

Vegetables will still need to be well cooked and mashed, though not necessarily blended to a purée. Your baby may well cope with small lumps of soft vegetables such as potato.

You can try introducing some more fruits such as kiwi fruit (seeds and all); fresh nectarines and peaches if in season, peeled and mashed; ripe mango; cherries (stoned and finely chopped); grapes.

Some berries, notably strawberries, can cause a reaction. Don't offer these to him until he is at least a year old.

Nuts and Seeds

Nuts and seeds can be added to the diet at this stage. They are a good source of protein and they contain fat soluble vitamins and useful minerals including calcium. Choose the milder varieties such as almonds, cashews, hazelnuts and sunflower seeds. Your baby's new ability to cope with coarse textures doesn't extend to nuts. They are too hard for his gums to deal with, and he can choke on small hard objects like these. You must use finely ground nuts. These can be added to mashed vegetable or fruit mixtures. Alternatively blend the ground nuts with some water to make nut creams and milks.

A variety of nut butters is available from health food shops. The key things to look for are those with no added sugar, those which are salt free or low salt, and smooth in texture.

Nut creams and milks can be made from almonds, cashews and sunflower seeds. Make sure the nut or seed is ground to a very fine powder first. Add about an equal quantity of water and blend very thoroughly. To make a milk, add more water gradually until the mixture has a consistency similar to normal cows' milk.

Pulses

The more easily digested pulses, such as lentils and split peas, can be given to young babies but it is essential that they are very well cooked. I feel it is best to pass the cooked mixture through a sieve to remove any hard pieces such as ungerminated seeds and the more fibrous outer skin. When first introducing pulses, start with a small quantity such as a dessertspoonful. The reason is that even with careful preparation, some babies cannot tolerate pulses until older. If they get a sore bottom after passing a motion, leave pulses out of the diet for another month or so. Once you are happy that your baby is able to digest the red lentils and yellow split peas you can introduce other pulses such as aduki beans, haricot beans and chick peas. These must all be thoroughly cooked and mashed well or puréed.

Red lentils and yellow split peas do not need soaking, simply pick them over for any ungerminated seeds or stones then wash well. Put in a pan using one part lentils to three parts water. Bring to the boil and simmer gently with the lid off until the mixture becomes quite thick. Stir several times during cooking. Press through a sieve so the mixture is quite smooth.

Aduki beans, haricot beans, chick peas need to be soaked overnight in plenty of water. Drain and rinse well. Bring to the boil in fresh water. Boil fiercely for ten minutes then simmer for 40 to 60 minutes until the bean is quite soft. Drain then mash well or purée.

Tofu is made from the soya bean and is suitable for babies of about eight months or more. Mash it straight into a vegetable or fruit purée. Alternatively, cook the tofu with the vegetables, a technique that works especially well in something like a tomato sauce.

Dairy Products

There is a continuing debate about the pros and cons of dairy products in infant diets. You should not introduce dairy products before six months. During the course of researching this book, advice on when to introduce them changed from around six months to 'maybe wait a year'. Your decision will depend upon your own history and your own baby. If anyone in your family has had a bad reaction to dairy products, suffering from asthma or eczema, for example, then wait until the baby is a year old.

Dairy products can be a useful part of a balanced diet. They are a good source of protein, rich in calcium and riboflavin (B_2) with smaller amounts of other vitamins and minerals, notably vitamin A (full fat milk only). They are versatile foods which can be used for both sweet and savoury dishes as well as snacks.

On the other hand dairy products have been thought to cause respiratory problems such as bronchitis. They are mucus forming foods that can lead to runny noses, sore throats, bronchitis and ear infections. They are a principle source of saturated fat. It is now thought by some that even in childhood eating dairy products can predispose a person to atherosclerosis, heart attacks and strokes.

In northern Europe, including Britain, it has been traditional to rely on milk quite heavily. In southern European countries much less is drunk and children there are just as healthy. Incidents of heart problems in adult life are also less, which may or may not be related.

Once you have decided to introduce dairy products, begin with processed products such as yoghurt or cheese; these are more easily digested. So too is plain milk which has been boiled and cooled. Some yoghurt has the added bonus of containing useful bacteria that help promote a healthy environment in the intestines. Choose those with BA cultures or Bio yoghurt. Sadly lots of yoghurt sold with children in mind has added sugar and often colouring and non-vegetarian gelatine. Whilst the bright packaging and latest cartoon character may be very appealing, it is surely better to avoid these and to make your own flavoured yoghurts. This is easy. Start with a plain yoghurt and flavour it with a home-made fruit purée. Dried fruits such as apricots are the best. If you make the fruit the dominant flavour, your baby will probably find the yoghurt mixture sweet enough. There is then no need for sugar or honey. You can add finely ground nuts, wheatgerm or muesli to make the yoghurt more substantial. Some babies will eat plain yoghurt quite happily.

Other dairy products to try are soft cheeses such as curd and cottage cheese. These can be mashed and mixed with fruit or vegetables. Hard cheese tends to have a high fat content and added salt, and can be quite hard to digest, so leave this until your baby is around a year old.

If you don't want to use cows' milk produce, there are many goats' milk alternatives on the market. Products such as goats' milk soft cheese and yoghurt are more easily digested than cows' milk.

If you do not give your baby any dairy products until your baby is a year old, be sure to monitor the amount of calcium in his diet. This mineral is critical for the baby's bones and teeth. Good sources of calcium are tofu, calcium enriched soya milks, pulses, nuts such as almonds, and oat flakes.

Egg white can cause allergies and it is wise not to use this part of the egg until the baby is a year old. The egg yolk (well cooked) may be tried, though you should still watch for any adverse reaction. An egg yolk is a rich source of iron. You can hard-boil an egg, then mash the yolk only into cooked vegetables. Egg yolks can also be used in baked dishes which you may make towards the end of your baby's first year.

Fats
After about six months, your baby will be able to digest a little fat. Don't aim to introduce too much into the diet, bearing in mind that one of the aims of healthy eating is not to have too high a percentage of fat in the diet. However, a little fat in the diet is useful as a source of the fat soluble vitamins. Small amounts of fat also aid digestion. Fat is a high calorie ingredient and can usefully bump up the calorie count of low calorie mixtures of plain vegetables. Olive oil, a mono-saturated fat which doesn't add to the cholesterol levels already in the blood, is the best to use. It is also easy to find unprocessed versions of this oil, sold as 'virgin'. Add up to a teaspoon of oil to a portion of food. A teaspoon is roughly forty calories.

Once your baby eats bread and rice cakes you may want a margarine. Look for margarines that do not have colours or salt added. These are generally available in health food shops and some supermarkets. An alternative is to use a good quality butter.

Herbs and Spices
As I mentioned, some babies will eat and enjoy things like garlic. They may eat a few herbs if mixed in with other foods. There isn't necessarily any nutritional value in this, it is simply that adding a few herbs may make the transition from baby food to sharing your meals easier. Spices are different. Hot spices such as chilli can irritate a young intestine and it is best not to use these until much later.

Texture and Consistency
During this period, your baby's ability to handle textures will change. He will graduate from the very soft liquid purées you made at the beginning to thicker drier mixtures and coarsely mashed food. When you try a new texture, your baby may not always take to it immediately. Persevere for a few spoonfuls to give him time to adjust. If it proves impossible, just wait a few more days.

From around six months babies get more interested in chewing (teeth or no teeth). As teeth develop, they will also want to bite on things. You can try large chunks of carrot or firm fruits such as apple or pear. Be aware that babies are quickly able to break off surprisingly large pieces. They will probably spit these out, but don't leave them alone with this sort of food because of the danger of choking.

Temperature

As with the first foods you introduced, there is no need for your baby's food to be hot. Room temperature is fine, though some sorts of meals, especially vegetable mixtures, do seem to go down better when warm. Food should still not be served cold straight from the fridge simply because your baby will probably not eat it.

How and When

During this second stage, start to put your baby into a high chair for meals, if you haven't done so already. Meal times will still be messy affairs. Early on the baby will probably enjoy reaching into the bowl and scrunching all the food between his fingers. Whilst this is not exactly good etiquette long term, it is all in the nature of exploring and learning to distinguish between different foods and how to eat them.

Babies also like to play with a spoon, maybe dipping it into the food but rarely being able to get this into their mouths until they are almost a year old, or even later. You can try giving them a spoon and guiding it into their mouths. It is a slow business. Babies will also learn the fun of letting go. This turns into the fun game of chucking a loaded spoon over the side of the chair. Have lots of newspapers or plastic sheets spread round – and aprons and bibs for you and the baby!

Your baby may be the type to sit and eat a meal all at one go. If this is the case, you can probably develop a routine of feeding three meals a day to a timetable that suits you both. Towards the latter part of the year you might make up a day's menu from the following foods.

Breakfast: half a banana, puréed apple or piece of fresh fruit. Cereal such as baby muesli, porridge, millet or puffed rice served with soya milk, cows' milk, diluted fruit juice or water. Fingers of toast with spread and sugar-free jam or marmalade.

Lunch and tea: use as your base a portion of cooked mixed vegetables (carrots, parsnips, potato, broccoli). Either steam or boil these or fry a little onion, add the vegetables and then the stock or sauce, and simmer until tender. Add protein and calories by serving these with one or two tablespoons of lentil or bean purée or nut butter plus a similar amount of mashed rice, bulgar wheat or pasta. Dairy products such as cottage cheese are also useful sources of protein; 50 g (2 oz) is about right. Pudding could be fresh fruit or a purée of dried fruit, such as apricots, mixed with yoghurt or fromage frais and a teaspoonful of ground nuts.

For snacks, offer rice cake or toast spread with yeast extract, sugar-free spread or half a tablespoon of nut butter, or fresh fruit.

Drinks can be soya milk or cows' milk, as much water as they like, and one drink of diluted fruit juice.

Ideas for Serving

As your baby is prepared to eat different textures, don't feel you need always to be serving bowls of mush. You can vary presentation in a number of ways.

- Serve the vegetables as separate portions coated in a white sauce or almond milk.
- Mix chopped vegetables with rice to make a mini-risotto.
- Bind vegetables with breadcrumbs and nut butter to make small burgers.
- Make a diced vegetable and tomato sauce to serve with pasta.
- Bake vegetables with a bean purée and an egg yolk to make a savoury bake.
- Top a mixture of vegetables with mashed potato and cover with a little grated cheese then lightly grill.
- Mash beans in a tomato sauce and serve on toast.
- Make a potato nest with mashed potato and cottage cheese and fill with cooked vegetables.
- Make a plain hummus with chick peas and tahini and a little garlic if your baby eats it. Serve with chopped skinned tomatoes, cucumber and pitta bread.
- Add chunks of tofu to a dish.

If your baby is the sort who likes constant small snacks and prefers eating on the go, then your goal is to get an adequate amount of useful nutrients eaten. To achieve this you might alter the daily menu I suggested previously and serve it in smaller quantities. For example, have the banana and cereal at breakfast, then the toast later in the morning.

As mentioned in the previous section, no baby is going to be quite the same in how they respond to food and how much they will eat. This will also vary on a day to day basis.

Even so, there are guidelines given on calorie intakes for this age group. Up to a year old baby boys are supposed to have 780 calories a day and girls 720. Bear in mind what sort of baby you have; larger, taller and heavier babies will need more calories. So, too, a baby who is walking before a year needs more than one who is perhaps only just getting mobile. The calorie requirement for children past their first birthday increases to 1200 for boys and 1100 for girls. I am sure the number doesn't change suddenly overnight but this gives an idea of what is right and how their needs increase. If you do sometimes feel that your baby is surviving on a very little it can be worth totting up the calories. As we know from calorie counted diets as an adult, it is surprising how they mount up.

Foods to Avoid

Towards the end of the first year, you are reaching a stage where your baby will eat more or less anything, depending on texture and temperature. Here is a reminder of the foods you should still avoid.
  Avoid foods they can choke on:
  • whole nuts
  • whole beans (those with a tough skin should be thoroughly mashed)
  • whole sultanas or raisins.
  Avoid foods that might trigger an allergy:
  • citrus fruits
  • strawberries
  • egg white
  • tea, coffee and alcohol

Stage 3: Weaning

The dictionary definition of weaning is 'to accustom to nourishment other than the mother's milk'. Weaning in this sense therefore starts from the moment you introduce solids and applies to the whole business of teaching the baby to eat. The last stage of weaning is ending the reliance on you for any food. So this section is to do with when and how to stop breast feeding and what to put in place of mother's milk.

If you are bottle feeding, this is a less complicated matter. You can keep on with formula milk for a year at least. Formula milk can be used to make puddings, purées and so on. Once you decide you would like to introduce ordinary milk or any other liquid, it is a matter of switching the contents of a bottle and seeing if it is acceptable. The transition should be fairly easy. Return to the usual drink if there seems to be any problem. Remember formula is fortified with iron and vitamins which is good for a baby with feeding difficulties.

If you are breast feeding, the process of weaning the baby away from you may be a little more involved. The baby not only enjoys sucking for the milk but he probably associates these times with comfort and security. Cuddling up to a hard plastic bottle doesn't have quite the same effect. This may make it difficult to introduce a bottle, or mean it is hard for the baby to give you up at all.

Don't try and go straight from four or five feeds a day to

nothing. This will be uncomfortable for you and more than a little disconcerting for the baby. Weaning away from the breast needs to be a gradual process rather like introducing solids. First watch for some signs from your baby. He may seem to want to suck less and be more interested in eating before drinking. Encourage this, plus offer him a drink, such as plain cooled boiled water, with his meals. Afterwards he may feel too full to want any more and automatically drop one of his feeds.

Various systems for giving drinks are available. With bottles and teats, there are several makes of teat that are supposed to resemble the nipple and to which your baby may find it easier to adjust. Ask your health visitor for advice. There is also a bottle system which consists of an outer shell which is then lined with a sterile plastic bag. That bag is then filled with whatever liquid you choose. One advantage is that the plastic bags are sold ready sterilised which saves you bother with bottle brushes and so on. This method is also convenient if you do a lot of travelling as it is easy to take along a roll of bags and several spare teats. Teats still need to be sterilised before use and rinsed with boiled water. Personally I found the best thing about this system was the fact that the baby doesn't have to tip the bottle back to drink from it. The sucking out of the bag works rather like a straw. This means the baby has a little independence early on and can take up the bottle when he wants during the day.

Another alternative is to move straight on to a training beaker or small cup. Training beakers are designed with thick spouts with three small holes through which the baby does a combination of sucking and drinking. Even when they discover how to shake the water out or throw the beaker off the high chair, not much gets spilt. If you want to use a cup, it is best to fill up something very small, such as a plastic egg cup, and let the baby learn drinking (and the effects of spilling) with this. Then move to a larger container when he has the right idea.

Don't feel you necessarily need to offer ordinary milk or a formula milk. The most important thing is for the baby to keep up his overall liquid intake so that he doesn't become constipated. A vegetarian diet does tend to contain more fibre than ordinary diets even at the baby stage. Fibre soaks up liquid which means it's essential your baby gets plenty to drink.

You can simply give cooled boiled water or very diluted fruit juices, such as orange or apple. Soya milk is also a possibility and this can be diluted according to your baby's taste. As the baby starts getting used to drinking quantities of other things and continuing to eat plenty, he may soon drop another feed. With many babies the midday feeds tend to go first, then the morning one, and lastly the night time feed, as this is probably the one where he needs the most comfort. Don't worry if your baby doesn't follow this pattern. In my case Ralph dropped his late night feed first.

Allowing your baby to stop feeding from you at his own pace is ideal. This gives you both time to adjust. If, however, you are the one who needs to give up feeding your baby for whatever reason (such as going back to work), you may end up dropping the feeds a little more quickly. This doesn't give your body time to get the message that you do not want to produce so much milk. You may well feel engorged, rather as you did when you first started feeding. If this happens, express a little milk so that you don't feel so swollen. It won't be as much as your baby might otherwise have drunk so your body will still get the message that you want to produce less.

The Question of Milk

In the good old days (when I was brought up!) the routine was to breast feed until six months and then move the baby straight on to milk from a cup. As already mentioned in this chapter, there is a wariness about introducing dairy products too early because of the risk of allergies. Approximately one in four people in the UK lack the enzyme to digest the sugar in milk. These undigested enzymes form mucus which can then lead to complaints such as sinusitis. Apart from the pros and cons mentioned on page 110, for some vegetarians and vegans there is also the moral dilemma over whether to eat milk and dairy products.

If you decide not to include dairy products, or only want to have your baby eating a little, make sure he has protein and calcium from other sources. Adequate protein is easily obtained from mixtures of grains, pulses and nuts. One of the best sources of calcium is enriched soya milk (the label should state whether calcium has been added). Other good sources are: almonds, hazelnuts, sunflower seeds, oatflakes; kale; chard; cabbage; red cabbage. There is also a small amount of calcium in leeks, carrots and dates.

Most health visitors and doctors recommend vitamins (in the form of drops) from about the time of weaning onto cow's milk or soya milk. These are not strictly necessary but can be useful if you have a faddy baby or one who's uninterested in food.

Stage 4: from about Twelve Months

From about a year old your child can virtually try all the foods you eat. Just have in mind the previous advice given about choking hazards until the toddler is two or three. You can simply serve portions of your own foods provided they are not highly spiced, heavily salted or very sweet. You may still need to alter the texture of some dishes by chopping or mashing the baby's portion especially when introducing a new ingredient. Be prepared still for inconsistencies. You may find that one day your baby is prepared to eat chunks of food, and another time will want more of a mash.

By the one year old stage, he may well be feeding himself pieces of bread, half a banana, a stick of carrot and so on. He may be soon able to manage a spoon quite efficiently though meals can be quite slow.

How to Continue into the Future

I hope that by following the advice in the previous sections, your baby will have got off to a good start in life and not only enjoy but be entirely accustomed to healthy meals and snacks as he enters toddlerhood.

Whatever your reasons for not eating meat or fish or cutting down on those foods, there is absolutely no reason why a child brought up thoughtfully on this sort of diet should not be as healthy as other children, or perhaps healthier. I say 'thoughtfully', as a vegetarian diet could consist of fizzy drinks and sweets which would be little use nutritionally at all.

Exactly the same rules for healthy eating apply to children as to adults. Aim to eat lots of cereals, grains and wholemeal bread, plenty of vegetables and fruit (both raw and cooked if your child is amenable). Fats such as margarine, butter and oil, and sugar (and therefore all the things containing sugar, such as cakes and biscuits) should have the least emphasis.

In terms of nutrients, children need smaller quantities of all the vitamins and minerals that adults need, except calcium. With calcium, the recommended daily allowance for children is the large figure of 600 mg. For adults it is 500 mg. You may worry about your child's protein intake, as protein is essential for growth. This concern is easily handled by including a variety of cereals, pulses, nuts and dairy produce on a daily basis in the diet. With this your baby should be getting ample amounts of the various proteins. As a guide to quantity the recommended daily allowance for one to two year olds is roughly half that of a sedentary adult.

Balance and variety are also very important. If your child eats lots of different things, you shouldn't need to feel worried as to whether he is getting all the nutrients. There will be times, of course, when your child is fussy and starts to refuse things. Try to find a nutritional substitute or if that doesn't work you may have to try and disguise what he doesn't like!

You may find it helpful to analyse your child's diet by food category. The target figures are very approximate so don't be worried by exact numbers. Of course, if you are using a vegan diet and excluding dairy produce you should probably check more carefully.

- Cereals: one serving is a slice of bread or several tablespoonfuls of muesli etc. Three servings per day are needed.
- Fruit: three or four pieces per day, including some citrus fruit, served chopped or as juice.
- Vegetables: one serving is a third of a cupful, a toddler needs two servings per day. Use either mixed vegetables or separate portions including some dark green or deep yellow vegetables (carrots, spinach, green pepper, broccoli).
- Protein foods such as beans, peas, lentils, tofu, nuts, seeds: one serving is several tablespoonfuls. Three servings per day are ideal.
- Dairy products (or substitute for vegans): one serving is a cup of milk, or a few pieces of cheese. Three servings per day.
- Fats: three teaspoonfuls a day as a spread or oil added to meals.

Healthy eating ideals should be fairly easy to keep up at home. As your baby gets older, joins play groups and toddler groups, it may be more difficult. Up to now, he has been fairly well protected from the outside world. As he enters more into society there will be many different pressures: well meaning adults offering treats of ice-cream and sweets, colourful packets, what they see others eating. To be frank, I think there is very little you can do except always have your own 'treats' on hand so that your child can be offered something along with everyone else.

Growing up as a Vegetarian

It is also as your baby starts to become more social that you may have to face up to questions about bringing up your child as a vegetarian. In recent years, many people have recognised the benefits of a vegetarian diet or the cruelties of a meat-eating one. It is also true that many children do not instantly like the taste of meat and they will probably enjoy tastes of the vegetarian meals you serve. I have found that most people are curious about the diet in a positive way, often looking for ideas for their own children and very rarely critical. Whether your own child will wish to remain vegetarian is impossible to tell.

Exercise and Relaxation

At one time, being pregnant meant you were advised to put your feet up for virtually nine months and do very little (assuming you could afford to). Recently opinion has changed and it is widely believed that a fit body has more strength and stamina to cope with the demands of pregnancy and childbirth. Tennis stars such as Evonne Cawley, athlete Liz McColgan and marathon runner Ingrid Kristiansen have shown you can still excel at a sport whilst pregnant or as a new mother. I'm not suggesting that we all have to win Wimbledon to have a healthy pregnancy but it is worth focusing on your own physical fitness and doing something if necessary to improve it.

This section looks at how to find a sport or activity you might enjoy. There are some suggestions on what to do if you have never done any exercise and what to take into account if you are considering exercising through your pregnancy. Whether you are already fit or not, there are also some specific exercises to help you in pregnancy.

After you have had the baby, exercise will help you recover and get back into shape more quickly. I've given some ideas to try postnatally.

At the end of the section there are some guidelines on how to relax as this is also important for your general well-being.

Pre-Pregnancy

This is the best time to take up a sport and get fitter. Nowadays there are all sorts of different leisure activities from which to choose. If you have never done any exercise, perhaps since leaving school, it can be a little daunting knowing where to start. It is best if your sport will fit into your lifestyle and be something you enjoy. It is not much good enthusiastically deciding to go to a regular dance class if you know that half the time you won't be able to get there, or taking up swimming if you can't bear the thought of ruining your hair each time it gets wet. You may want something you can do from your front door (jogging, running, cycling), something inside (keep fit, dance), team sports (hockey, rowing), something gentle (yoga, tai chi). To find out more about sports in your area you can contact your library, your local borough council (many of whom have recreation officers), or the sports council who can give you addresses of national sports bodies who may have representatives in your area.

If you do take up a sport, don't expect too much of yourself too quickly. Even taking things slowly can mean an enormous amount of improvement in a few months.

Once You Are Pregnant

If you are used to exercising, there is no reason not to continue this through your pregnancy. You must, of course, stop if you feel any unusual pain or discomfort. I found as a regular runner that during the first three months when I had expected to be able to exercise without any problem, tiredness and nausea meant I didn't feel like doing much training. However, once that passed, I felt fine. At four and a half months I ran a half-marathon and at five months competed in the British Orienteering championships. I stopped running seriously at six months, but managed a little jogging and lots of walking until the day before Ralph was born.

Continuing with your regular programme has many advantages. It should stop you putting on excess weight and improve energy levels. You may reduce the possibility of peripheral oedema (swelling of the hands and ankles). Exercise will improve your circulation and may relieve constipation, prevent varicose veins and avoid cramp. It can also help you unwind and you may get a better night's sleep.

Late on in pregnancy, your own physical condition may stop you doing so much. Your balance may be affected as you increase in size, you may need to go to the loo more often, and you may simply feel self-conscious. Do be aware of this and adapt your activities accordingly.

If you are intending to carry on with your sport here are some guidelines to follow:

- Check with your doctor first and continue to be advised through pregnancy.
- Only do what you consider appropriate, and expect to taper off in the last three months.
- Always warm up properly before you start and allow yourself time to cool down.
- Avoid over-heating. Try to exercise in cool weather, or at cool times of day.

- Be careful not to get dehydrated. Drink before, during and afterwards, as necessary.
- Maintain adequate weight gain.

Apart from their own well-being, pregnant women may be concerned as to the effect of exercise on the growing foetus. It is reassuring to know that injury to the foetus is very rare; generally it has to be caused by something as traumatic as a car accident.

There are a number of reasons why the foetus is safe. Until the twelfth week of gestation, the uterus is well protected by the bones of the pelvis. Only after that does it enlarge into the abdomen where it is more vulnerable. Even so, the foetus is well cushioned by the thick spongy layers of the uterus and approximately a litre of amniotic fluid. When you move, the effect on the foetus is rather like an egg being shaken in a jar of water. The liquid cushions and protects the egg even when shaken vigorously. The egg can really only come to harm if the jar is broken.

If you have not taken any exercise and find you are pregnant, this is not the time to start anything demanding. There are, however, some easy ways to improve your overall fitness.

Try to do more walking. Walk briskly rather than dawdle. Try to walk purposefully for at least fifteen to thirty minutes a minimum of three times a week.

Recreational swimming (rather than powering up and down the pool lanes) will help you tone your muscles safely. Try to go once or twice a week. Many areas also run antenatal swimming lessons where you can learn about exercises to do in the pool. These can be fun as the water takes some of your weight.

Concentrate, too, on improving your posture. Think of yourself standing tall, keeping your shoulders and neck relaxed and your back long. Tuck your tail bone underneath you. Try to do this when you are talking on the telephone or standing in the supermarket queue. It will tone your muscles and soon become a habit.

Make time to do the antenatal exercises!

Antenatal Exercises

Whatever your state of fitness, it is worth doing some specific exercises during pregnancy. These are designed to strengthen areas that will be affected by the extra weight you are carrying and stretch some muscles that can help when giving birth. Having more bodily awareness and control may assist you during labour. These exercises can also reduce tension.

Before starting on the exercises, however, it is vital to learn about the pelvic floor and how to strengthen it.

The Pelvic Floor

Many women will never have heard of a pelvic floor, let alone thought of exercising it. It is one of the muscles that can be most affected during pregnancy and childbirth. If the pelvic floor becomes weak, you may suffer from minor incontinence – a small leak of urine if you sneeze, cough or laugh suddenly. You may not be able to exercise or even run for the bus without worrying. Some women also find that a weak pelvic floor lessens their enjoyment of sex.

The pelvic floor is rather like a hammock of muscles slung below the pelvis joining the pubic bone at the front and the spine at the back. These muscles support the womb, bladder and bowels. The pelvic floor is shaped in a figure of eight with a larger loop controlling the outlets of the urethra and vagina, and a smaller ring of muscle to the back which controls the anal sphincter. The two rings of muscle overlap in the centre which is called the perineum.

During pregnancy there is an increase of the hormone relaxin. This softens ligaments and tissues, allowing the joints of the body to stretch more easily to accommodate your growing baby. The muscles of the pelvic floor are also softened. In addition, the extra weight of the baby in the uterus may weaken the muscles.

During childbirth the pelvic floor needs to relax and stretch to make room for the baby to emerge through the vaginal opening. It can help if you are aware of this muscle and able to relax it, as this can lessen the risk of a tear.

During your pregnancy and afterwards it is very important to strengthen this muscle to save you discomfort afterwards and give you confidence. The following exercises are probably the least strenuous, but consider them among the most important you do. The movement you are looking for is only small. Repetition is the key to success. Once you have the idea, try to do fifty a day (though more won't do you any harm).

First you need to identify this muscle. Try stopping yourself mid-flow when urinating, hold for a count of four, then let your bladder empty out completely. Remember how you did this (it may take a few goes), then repeat the action without passing water and hold for four.

Other things to try to make you more aware of this muscle are to imagine holding in a tampon (in other words tightening the muscles of the vagina). Alternatively, imagine being desperate to pee and having a touch of diarrhoea all at the same time and how you would control that!

Once you feel you are aware of the muscle try the following exercise. Lie on your back with your knees bent up. Have your feet on the floor about hip width apart. Keep the top half of your body relaxed. Use a pillow under your head if you prefer. Focus on the area around your vagina. Try to imagine lifting the pelvic floor muscle in stages as if going up in a lift stopping briefly on each floor. Then repeat the process in small stages in reverse, letting the muscle relax. Always finish the exercise by pulling the muscle up slightly. Do this exercise at least ten times, more if possible.

Once you are able to do this well, try the same thing in a standing or sitting position. Then get into the habit of doing at least fifty tightenings each day – at the sink, waiting at traffic lights, queuing in shops, doing the ironing – anywhere. You won't regret it.

Other Exercises

Apart from getting into a habit of exercising your pelvic floor, it is worth finding some time to do a few other exercises. The aim of these exercises are to work on specific areas of the body that are affected during pregnancy. You need some parts, such as the pelvis and the spine, to become more mobile and other areas, such as the legs and buttocks, to become stronger to cope with your increasing weight. I feel it is worth concentrating on a few exercises and doing those thoroughly. These are then easy to repeat and remember. Take the exercises slowly, being conscious where appropriate of stretching your body. Don't hold your breath. Just breathe easily and evenly throughout.

Loose comfortable clothing is fine. You'll perhaps feel more encouraged to do the exercises if you don't have to change into anything special. Bare feet are best. As a general warm up, dance around to a favourite record or piece of music. Let your arms swing, move your head from side to side, bend your knees, pick your feet up off the floor, swing your hips a little like a gentle version of the twist or slow motion Hula-Hoop.

Stand Tall

Stand with your feet slightly apart, with your weight balanced evenly between them. Feel your feet are firmly fixed to the floor. Think tall, with the stretch coming up through your legs and lifting your stomach muscles. Imagine your spine is long, it extends through the crown of your head, lengthening your neck. Tuck your tail bone (the base of the spine) underneath you by tightening the muscles under your buttocks. Keep your arms and your face relaxed.

Good posture helps you lengthen your spine and gives your baby more room. Standing tall means you lift your abdominal muscles, thereby keeping them toned.

Side Stretch

Standing with feet about a metre apart, raise the left arm to one side and then over the head to the right as far as is comfortable. Feel the stretch on the left side. Put the other hand on your hip if that is easier. Hold for eight counts, breathing easily, then return to the starting position. Repeat on the other side.

Spinal Twist

Stand with your feet hip width apart. Bend your knees. Hold your arms straight in front of you at shoulder level, lightly crossed. Gently twist round to look behind you, first one way, then the other.

Hip Rolls
Stand with your feet slightly apart, knees
a little bent. Push your hip to one side
then the other side. Repeat. Make large
circles with the pelvis, rather like doing
the Hula-Hoop in slow motion. Repeat
in the opposite direction.

This exercise makes you aware of your
pelvis, which may help you carry the weight
of your baby better and means you can make
yourself more comfortable in childbirth.

Repeat those three exercises once more, or
several times if you wish. Then stand with
your back to a wall for the next group of exercises.

Pelvic Tilt
Have your back against the wall and your feet
about 15 cm (6 in) away. Bend your knees.
Press the small of your back into the wall and
at the same time tip your pelvis bone upwards
so that your bottom leaves the wall. Then
relax and repeat.

This helps your awareness of the pelvic
area and helps counteract the tilt forward
that comes later in pregnancy due to the
extra weight.

Calf Stretch
Standing a little further from the wall, face
towards it. Take a step towards the wall
with the right leg, keeping it bent.
Concentrate on stretching the left heel
towards the floor. Repeat with the
other leg.

This will help the calf stretch
and should make squatting easier.

Squatting
Stand about 45 cm (18 in) away from the
wall with your feet 45 cm (18 in) apart.
Use your hands against the wall to give
you balance. Go down into a squat. Hold
for fifteen seconds or longer. Then use your
hands to help you stand. Remember to
stand tall.

   Aim to practise squatting for longer.
This strengthens the legs and helps stretch
the inner thigh. It may also be a position you adopt in labour.

Repeat these three exercises if you wish.

The Cat
Kneel on all fours, keeping your spine
straight. Pull in your buttocks
so that your spine arches,
then straighten out. Do not
arch the other way. Repeat.
This is another version of the pelvic lift. It will help strengthen
your stomach and buttock muscles which in turn support
the weight of your trunk. Strength in this area may help prevent
lower back strain.

Spinal Twist
Kneel on all fours and
slowly look behind you to
one side. Repeat.

The Bridge
Ease yourself on to your
back. Put a pillow under
your head if you wish. Keep
your knees bent, feet on the
floor, hip width apart. Lift
your hips off the ground until

your back is in a straight line from your shoulders. Feel that you
lift the pubic bone first, tightening the buttock muscles as you
lift. Lower your hips back to the floor. Curl on to one side and
then use your arms to push up to a sitting position.
This exercise strengthens your buttocks which helps you
carry the extra weight of your pregnancy.

The Butterfly
Sitting with soles of the feet together, make sure your back is straight. You may need to support yourself with your hands either side, or sit on a few pillows. Let your knees fall out as much as possible. Close your eyes and breathe in and out. As you breathe out try to feel the legs (inner thighs) relaxing even more. Do not strain.

This helps stretch the inner thigh which in turn makes squatting easier.

Repeat these four exercises if you wish. Continue with the following exercises if you have time.

Ankle Rotations
Rotating your ankles, either while sitting or holding on to a chair. Also point and flex your feet.

This helps the circulation and may prevent you from getting cramp.

Shoulder Circles
Put the tips of your fingers on your shoulders. Move your elbows in a circle backwards. Make ten circles then relax.

This exercise may release tension in the shoulders. It helps counteract the weight of the pregnancy pulling you forward.

Postnatal Exercises

Although it may be the last thing you feel like after giving birth, exercise will help your recovery. I was dozing in the ward the day after Ralph was born when the physiotherapist visited and urged all us new mothers into action – only of the most gentle sort. I remember thinking 'exercise – already' and relishing the comfortable bed and my sleepy state.

Your body will start readjusting immediately after the birth, though the process is slow. Start as soon as you feel able. In the short term, exercises can boost your circulation and help the healing process. Doing exercises can be morale boosting as your waistline shrinks and you fit into your pre-pregnancy wardrobe. In the longer term, they help your stamina, so necessary with a young baby.

It's a great feeling if on the first day you only manage one or two repeats to find how soon you work your way up to ten. You may not feel entirely back to normal for three months or longer. You may get your figure back this quickly but softened ligaments take time to firm up. I still found it more comfortable when sleeping on my tummy to have a pillow under my hips and that was ten months after having Ralph.

For the first two weeks, concentrate on gently exercising the two areas of the body that need special attention immediately: your tummy and your pelvic floor.

Pelvic Floor

If you have familiarised yourself with the pelvic floor before the birth, try doing some straightforward tightening. As you get stronger you can go on to the imaginary lift exercise described on page 124. Start with ten repetitions and then build up to doing a few more each day.

Abdomen

This will be baggy after the birth. For a quick reference, here are the three exercises you can start straight away.

Pelvic Tilt
Lie on your back with your knees bent and your feet on the floor. Press the small of your back into the floor using the abdominal
muscles, rather like trying to do up the zip on a tight pair of trousers. Hold for a count of four then release. Repeat.

Small Side Bends
Lie flat on the bed, knees
bent, feet flat, arms by your
sides. Reach a little way with
the right hand towards the
right foot, then return to the
straight position and reach with the left hand to the left foot.

Diagonal Reach
Lie flat on the bed with your
knees bent and feet flat.
Reach with the right hand
across the body to the left
knee. The head and shoulder
only just come off the bed. Breathe out on exertion.

Checking your Abdominal Muscles

It is a good idea to check your abdominal muscles. These consist of four interlacing layers of muscle which help to protect internal organs as well as aid bodily movement. In the middle of the abdomen, however, the muscle which runs up and down the centre is only one layer thick. It consists of two muscles side by side which in pregnancy separate to make room for the baby. It does take some time for the gap to close. It is important not to do too strenuous abdominal exercise before this gap has closed. The wider the gap, the weaker your stomach muscles and it is all to easy to strain inadvertently.

To check the gap, lie on your back with your knees bent. Lift your head off the floor and reach with one hand towards your foot. With the other hand feel the stomach muscles just below your navel. There will probably be a gap between the two ridges of muscle. It may be between one and six centimetres wide. As the muscle strength improves, the gap should eventually narrow to just a finger tip width.

After Two Weeks

After about ten days your stitches may have healed or have disappeared. If you had bruising this should have eased. Overall you will probably be feeling somewhat stronger. You can try some of the exercises you did before the birth. In addition, do some more toning exercises for the stomach and for the buttocks. Always start your exercises with a gentle warm up such as moving freely to a piece of music.

Stand Tall
Reach up. Keeping the same
position as when you stand
tall, simply reach with one
hand straight above your
head. Repeat.

Side Bends
Keeping the lifting feeling
you had in the previous
exercise, put your hands on
your hips, and, keeping your
knees slightly bent, bend first
one way and then the other.

Spinal Twist
This time, keep the lower
body still, do a pelvic tilt
then gently twist the upper
body one way, back to the
centre, then the other way.

Pelvic Tilt
(Page 129.)

Straight Curl Up
Lie flat on your back with
your knees bent and feet flat.
Have a pillow under your
head if you wish. Breathe
out as you reach towards
your knees by curling your head and shoulders forward. Don't
let your tummy bulge out. (If this happens you may be trying to
lift too far.) Then roll back. As you get stronger, do without the
pillow.

Small Side Bends
(Page 130.)

Diagonal Reach
(Page 130.)

Leg Sliding
Lie on your back with your knees
bent and feet flat. Do a pelvic
tilt then let one leg
straighten, being sure to
keep the small of your back
pressed down. Draw the leg back up and repeat with the other
leg. As you get stronger you can do both legs together.

The Cat
(Page 127.)

Ankle Rotations
(Page 128.)

Shoulder Circles
(Page 128.)

Neck Circles
Looking to one side, down, then
up to the other side.

After Six Weeks

Six weeks after the birth you should have a doctor's appointment to check your postnatal progress. The doctor may check your blood pressure, urine and weight. If you had stitches you may be examined to see if they have healed. The doctor will also see if your uterus is back to its normal size.

Continue with your exercise programme adding a few variations if you now feel you have the stamina to deal with these.

| *Stand Tall* (Page 125.) | *Side Stretch* (Page 125.) | *Spinal Twist* (Page 125.) | *Hip Rolls* (Page 126.) |

Curl Down

Sitting with your legs out in front of you and knees slightly bent, start by pulling in your abdomen and tilting your pelvis. Then lean back until you feel a tightening in the stomach muscles. Hold for a second or two then return to sitting.

Pelvic Tilts
(Page 129.)

Curl Up

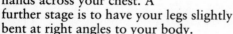

To make curl ups more difficult once your stomach is stronger, try holding your hands across your chest. A further stage is to have your legs slightly bent at right angles to your body.

Diagonal Curl Up

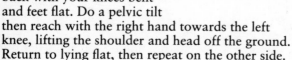

This is an extension of the diagonal reach. Lie on your back with your knees bent and feet flat. Do a pelvic tilt then reach with the right hand towards the left knee, lifting the shoulder and head off the ground. Return to lying flat, then repeat on the other side.

The Bridge
(Page 127.)

This next series of exercises helps stretch both the legs and strengthen the stomach muscles. Just start with the first two and work up to more as you feel ready.

Knee up to Chest
Lie on your back with your legs outstretched. Lift one leg up to your chest with the knee bent and hug it with your arms. Relax and repeat with the other leg.

Thigh Stretch
Lie on your back, bend your knees and keep your feet flat. Lift the right leg and put the right ankle on the left knee. Put both hands behind the left thigh and stretch it towards you. Feel a stretch in the right buttock. Relax and repeat with the other leg.

Leg Rolls
Still on your back, bring both legs up and roll them over to one side in a controlled way, keeping your shoulders on the floor, then roll them to the other side, breathing out on exertion. This exercise takes some effort so go carefully at the first attempt.

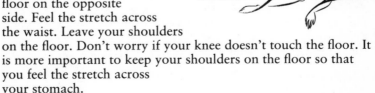

Waist Stretch
Lift one leg up as in the first exercise, then let it drop over your body to reach the floor on the opposite side. Feel the stretch across the waist. Leave your shoulders on the floor. Don't worry if your knee doesn't touch the floor. It is more important to keep your shoulders on the floor so that you feel the stretch across your stomach.

The Cat
(Page 127.)

Cat Stretch
On all fours, stretch one leg
out behind, then relax.
Repeat with the other leg.

Quads Stretch
Standing tall, lift one leg behind you,
bending at the knee. Hold your ankle
not your foot. Gently pull the lower
half of the leg towards you. You should
feel a stretch down the front of the
thigh.

Half Press Up
Kneel on all fours with your
hands shoulder width apart,
fingers pointing forwards.
Keeping your back straight,
lower yourself to the floor
by bending your elbows
outwards until your face is a few centimetres from the floor.
Then return to the starting position.

Ankle Rotations
(Page 128.)

Shoulder Circles
(Page 128.)

Triceps
Sitting up, stretch both arms above the
head, bend your right arm at the elbow,
then put your left hand on your right
elbow and push slightly so that you feel
a stretch down the back of the right
arm. Repeat on the other side.

Aerobic Exercise

Apart from these exercises, you may feel strong enough now to take up some aerobic exercise. This will very much depend on your fitness beforehand.

Aerobics have had a mixed press. There was the initial enthusiasm in the seventies when this form of exercise seemed so exciting and dynamic compared to traditional keep fit classes. Then it seemed that all this 'going for the burn' could lead to abnormal bodily stress and possible injury. Any exercise should be completed well before the point of collapse. It should be emphasised, however, that aerobic exercise isn't confined to the exercise studio. Aerobic literally means 'with oxygen'. This type of exercise increases the amount of oxygen the body can process within a given time (aerobic capacity) and that depends on having a good cardiovascular system. The cardiovascular system comprises the heart, the arteries and veins, the tiny tubes in the muscles and the blood. The better the cardiovascular system, the better the aerobic capacity. The system can be improved through aerobic exercise as the heart, like any other muscle, responds to exercise. By exercising aerobically you build up muscle tone, improve circulation and increase stamina.

Exercise such as brisk walking, gentle jogging, swimming lengths and cycling are all aerobic. Doing a little of these exercises will help your general fitness.

After Six Weeks

It is often more fun doing exercises in a group and you may find postnatal exercise classes advertised at your local baby clinic or GP's surgery. Sometimes these are run by NCT groups. Postnatal exercise classes usually include a warm up sequence, a short aerobic session (low impact – that is no jumping) and some specific toning of areas such as the stomach and bottom. The classes often finish with a relaxation session and sometimes a discussion on issues relevant to new mothers. Babies are always welcome and can sometimes be involved.

After Three to Four Months

You should be able to resume your normal sport or activity at this time. Do be sure that the teacher or instructor knows you have recently had a baby.

Relaxation

Relaxation is just as vital as exercise in contributing to your overall sense of well-being. There are bound to be times during your pregnancy and after the birth when you get tense, tired or both. The more you can learn to relax the more quickly you can shed these feelings. Relaxation will be useful in labour. If you are tense you will be using up vital energy that you might need to give birth. Labour can be a stressful experience and the more you are able to relax, the better you'll cope.

Relaxation is different from just resting. Contradictory as it may sound, you do need to make a conscious effort to relax; it is not a matter of putting your feet up for a rest. That is enjoyable, true, but usually the whole of you, mentally and physically, doesn't switch off completely. I remember learning relaxation techniques in a draughty church hall near Scarborough, with the clink of tea-making in the background and a busy road just outside the front door. Not the best place to relax, but about as challenging as a labour ward.

If you go to yoga classes you will probably learn some relaxation exercises. It is not that easy to learn relaxation from a book. If this is your only alternative, either ask your partner or a friend to read out the following paragraphs until you're very familiar with what to do, or you could read out the instructions yourself on to a tape and then finish with some peaceful music. This sequence I use to relax is a mixture of drama techniques and visualisation for relaxing the mind, and the contrast of tension and release to relax the body.

First, find a comfortable way of lying on the floor, propped up with pillows if you wish. If you prefer, sit in a chair that you find comfortable.

I find the best way to relax is to tense each part of the body first as this makes you focus on that area and consciously relax it. Begin with the feet and toes. Make them tense, perhaps scrunching up the toes, then let the muscles go. Then tense the shins, calves and ankles. Push hard into your heels, flexing the feet, then relax the muscles completely. Next contract the thighs and buttocks. Feel that the muscles are firm and solid, then let them go. Next the waist, abdomen and rib cage – tense and let go. Continue with the hands, either making a fist or spreading the fingers out as far as possible, then let the hands relax completely. Then tense the whole arm, and let those muscles relax. Next tense the shoulder girdle and spine, then let the muscles go. Then the neck and relax. Finally tense the face. Make an expression such as an exaggerated grin or deep scowl. Feel the inside of the mouth tensing. Scrunch up your eyes too. Relax all the face, including the tongue, jawbone and eyes. Take a few deep breaths almost like sighs then continue to breathe normally. Try to feel that your whole body is very heavy. If you are on the floor, imagine sinking into the floor or spreading over it like a pool of water. If you are sitting in a chair, feel as though you sink further down into the chair as though almost becoming part of it.

Then is the time to relax your mind. First you need to stop your mind racing, thinking about wall papering the nursery or cooking enough bean casserole to fill the freezer. A good method is to concentrate on listening to any sounds you can hear outside the room, perhaps the noise of traffic, wind in the trees, an aeroplane overhead, a church clock chiming. Then turn your attention to the sounds inside the room: perhaps there is a clock ticking, the hum of central heating, your own breathing. After a while, just listen to your own breathing and be aware of its rhythm. See if you can imagine the air flowing in and out of a dark tunnel. You are in this tunnel and are going to walk out into a landscape where you feel completely at ease. It could be somewhere by the sea, a beautiful garden, a shady wood, a lonely hill top. Wherever you can see, feel quite at ease. The temperature is just right, the air surrounding you feels very soft as it washes over your body. Feel that the light around you is soft. Think about that light and imagine basking in a warm gentle glow. Think of words such as soft, light, warm, gentle. Allow yourself the time to rest here. Gradually let the soft light fade until you are back in the dark tunnel listening and feeling your own breathing. Become conscious again of the outside world, the sounds in and out of the room. Gently stretch out your body, first wiggling your toes and fingers, then moving your legs and arms, your face next and then your body. Take your time sitting up or coming to standing.

This sequence of relaxing probably takes ten to fifteen minutes. Depending on how you feel and what time you are able to get to yourself, try to relax two or three times a week, every day if possible.

Recipes

This section contains some thirty recipes as well as lots of tips which I hope will be the basis of some simple nutritious cookery for you both during and after pregnancy.

Topics I've covered included light snacks, main meals, wholesome puddings and cakes, better breakfasts and sandwich fillings. Most of these ideas are suitable for pre- and post-pregnancy. I've included ingredients that are particularly useful from a nutritional point of view, such as green vegetables, high fibre foods, low fat dairy produce and tofu, as well as suggesting recipes with good protein combinations.

I've pointed out if a dish is suitable for freezing (for up to three months) so if you have spare time and energy you can fill your freezer.

Where possible, I've also suggested ways to adapt these recipes for your own baby once he starts to eat a wider range of foods after 6 months or so. I hope this will help you see how your own food can be easily adapted for your little one.

If you are looking for more ideas, there are plenty of suitable recipes in my book, *Sarah Brown's Quick and Easy Vegetarian Cookery*, also published by BBC Books.

SOUPS

Soups are useful both as snacks eaten on their own or for making light meals more substantial. Serve them with bread, sandwiches or baked potatoes.

Vegetarian foods lend themselves well to soups as most mixtures of vegetables can be combined to make a broth, whilst beans and grains provide texture and extra nutrients. A tin of tomatoes and tomato purée or a good stock will improve the flavour. Alter the texture either by blending only a part rather than all of the soup.

A thermos of soup makes a good lunch if you are taking food out. With this in mind the three recipes I have included are smooth and of a pouring consistency.

Carrot Soup with Rice

This is a light yet nutritious soup which is easy to make. It can also be made with barley if you prefer. This will make it a little thicker and you may have to add a little extra stock or water when processing. This recipe, without the seasoning, is suitable for babies once they are at the stage of eating combinations of foods. Sometimes a soup is useful if they are teething or unwell when often they seem to want meals that are quite liquid.

*This recipe is suitable for freezing.

SERVES 4

---

1 tablespoon oil
1 onion, peeled and finely chopped
2 sticks celery, sliced
350 g (12 oz) carrot, peeled and diced
100 g (4 oz) mushrooms
50 g (2 oz) brown rice
1 litre (1³/₄ pints) stock
2 tablespoons chopped fresh parsley
Seasoning

Heat the oil and fry the onion and celery until soft. Add the carrots and mushrooms and cook for 5 minutes or until just beginning to soften. Add the rice, stir well, then pour over the stock and add the parsley. Bring to the boil, then cover and simmer for 45 minutes until the rice and vegetables are thoroughly cooked. Leave to cool, then blend in a food processor or blender until smooth. Season to taste. Re-heat before serving.

•

Watercress and Potato Soup

Watercress is a good source of iron and vitamin C. In this recipe it is scarcely cooked so it retains as many nutrients as possible. If you prefer a cold soup, you can add yoghurt or fromage frais to the finished soup once it has cooled. Then chill well before serving. This soup is suitable for babies if you omit the seasoning. As the flavour is quite strong, you can mash in some plain cooked vegetables.
  *This recipe is suitable for freezing without the yoghurt.

SERVES 4

1 tablespoon oil
1 onion, peeled and chopped
1 leek, trimmed and chopped
225 g (8 oz) potatoes, peeled, and diced
900 ml (1¹/₂ pints) vegetable stock
1 tablespoon shoyu
1 bunch of watercress
Seasoning

Heat the oil and gently fry the onion and leek until soft. Add the potatoes and cook briefly. Pour over the stock and shoyu and bring to the boil. Cover the pan and cook for 30 minutes. Using a food processor, purée the watercress until all the leaves are finely chopped. Then pour over the soup and purée again until the soup is smooth. Do not over-blend or the potatoes become glutinous. Season to taste. Return to the heat and warm through before serving.

•

Yellow Split Pea Soup with Herbs

This nutritious and filling soup could be made with a variety of root vegetables. Split peas may be one of the first pulses you try out on your baby and the smooth texture of this soup should be ideal.
  *This recipe is suitable for freezing.

SERVES 4

*1 tablespoon oil
1 onion, peeled and finely chopped
2 sticks celery, trimmed and chopped
350 g (12 oz) parsnips, peeled and diced
100 g (4 oz) yellow split peas, washed
1 teaspoon fresh thyme, chopped
1 teaspoon fresh sage, chopped
1.2 litres (2 pints) stock or water
1 tablespoon tomato purée
Seasoning*

Heat the oil and gently fry the onion until soft. Add the celery and cook for a few minutes then add the parsnips and split peas. Mix in the fresh herbs and pour over the stock or water. Stir in the tomato purée. Bring to the boil then simmer for 50 to 60 minutes or until the peas are thoroughly cooked. Leave the soup to cool, then liquidise until completely smooth. Season to taste. Return to the pan and re-heat gently before serving.

•

MAIN COURSES

I've chosen ten simple main meal ideas that are designed to get you through a couple of weeks (minus the weekends when you may have help and more time to think if nothing else).

Baked Aduki Burgers

This is an ideal recipe to make if you have cooked beans and vegetables on hand. The mixture is quite soft and shaping the burgers needs to be done carefully. Baking the burgers in the oven saves you the bother of frying, and the worry of them falling apart. Babies of eight months upwards will probably enjoy these if well mashed with other vegetables or chopped into small pieces for them to have as finger food. Eventually you can serve them in a bun! This recipe also works well with black-eyed beans. It is worth cooking 450 g (1 lb) aduki (or black-eyed) beans at a time. Soak them overnight or for several hours. Then boil them for 10 minutes in fresh water and simmer for 40 to 50 minutes or until soft. Drain and freeze or use immediately.

*This recipe is suitable for freezing.

MAKES 12

175 g (6 oz) cooked aduki beans
350 g (12 oz) cooked vegetables
2 tablespoons tomato purée
2 tablespoons nut butter (cashew, sesame or peanut)
2 tablespoons chopped fresh parsley
1 tablespoon shoyu
225 g (8 oz) breadcrumbs
Seasoning
Wholewheat flour for shaping the burgers

Pre-heat the oven to gas mark 5, 190° C (375°F).

Put all the ingredients, except the breadcrumbs, seasoning and flour into a food processor and blend well. Add up to 225 g (8 oz) of breadcrumbs until the mixture is firm enough to shape. Season to taste. Using a little wholewheat flour, shape the mixture into 12 burgers. Place on an oiled baking sheet and bake in the oven for 10 to 15 minutes on each side.

•

Barley Hot Pot

Barley is a useful grain as it will thicken any liquid in which it is cooked as well as adding a good texture and flavour. In this recipe I've cooked it with root vegetables and a rich stock. Serve this hot pot on its own, rather like a substantial soup, or with green vegetables and mashed or baked potato. Your baby should enjoy this provided the barley is well cooked and very soft. You can mash the vegetables or not as you wish.

*This recipe is suitable for freezing.

SERVES 4

---

1 tablespoon sunflower oil
1 onion, chopped
2 leeks, trimmed and chopped
1 parsnip, chopped
2 carrots, chopped
250 g (8 oz) chopped swede
125 g (4 oz) green beans, trimmed and chopped
125 g (4 oz) barley
900 m (1¹/₂ pints) stock
1 teaspoon yeast extract
1 tablespoon tomato purée
2 tablespoons fresh parsley, chopped
1 bay leaf
Seasoning

Heat the oil and gently fry the onion. Add the vegetables and cook for five to seven minutes, stirring occasionally. Add the barley, stir in, then pour over the stock and stir in the yeast extract, tomato purée and herbs. Bring to the boil, then cover and simmer for 50 to 60 minutes, stirring occasionally and adding more water if necessary. The hot pot is ready when the barley is tender and the liquid reduced and well thickened. Season to taste.

•

Black-eyed Bean and Bulgar Casserole

Tinned black-eyed beans and bulgar wheat make this a simple nutritious casserole. Serve it with a side salad, steamed carrots or Red Cabbage with Walnuts and Soured Cream (page 148) for a more substantial meal. Once your baby is happily eating pulses (from nine to twelve months), you can mash up portions of this recipe to make a meal. Although the spices are quite mild, it is best to reduce the amount used until the baby is over a year.

*This recipe is suitable for freezing.

SERVES 4

1 tablespoon sunflower oil
1 onion, peeled and chopped
1 aubergine, diced
1 teaspoon garam masala
1 teaspoon paprika
1 red pepper, de-seeded and chopped
50 g (2 oz) chestnut mushrooms, chopped
50 g (2 oz) green beans, chopped
1 × 300 g (11 oz) tin black-eyed beans, drained
50 g (2 oz) bulgar wheat
2 tablespoons tomato purée
600–900 ml (1–1¹/₂ pints) vegetable stock
Seasoning

Pre-heat the oven to gas mark 5, 190°C (375°F).

Heat the oil and gently fry the onion until soft. Add the aubergine and cook until soft, adding a little more oil if necessary. Add the spices and cook for 2 minutes. Then add in the remaining ingredients except the tomato purée and stock. Stir well. Pour over the stock then add the tomato purée. Mix thoroughly and bring to the boil. Transfer to the oven and casserole for 1–1¼ hours or simmer in a covered pan for 40 to 50 minutes. Season to taste.

•

Creamed Pasta

Soya milk makes an excellent white sauce which can be used for vegetables or with pasta as in this very simple supper dish. Do serve this recipe with some colourful side vegetables such as grilled tomatoes or creamed spinach and you will have a tasty, healthy meal. Your baby may enjoy this dish with the ingredients mashed or chopped to suit.

This recipe is not suitable for freezing.

SERVES 4

50 g (2 oz) margarine
25 g (1 oz) wholewheat flour
1 pint soya milk (unsweetened)
350–450 g (12–16 oz) wholewheat macaroni
2–3 tablespoons chopped fresh parsley
Seasoning

Melt the margarine, then add the flour and mix to a roux and cook for 2 to 3 minutes. Pour over the milk, stirring constantly, and bring to the boil. Add the parsley and simmer for 3 to 4 minutes. Season well. Meanwhile, cook the pasta in plenty of boiling, salted water until tender. Drain, mix in the sauce and serve hot.

•

Lentil and Sesame Bake

Lentils are a quick-cooking pulse that provide a good source of iron. In this recipe they are made into a simple loaf that can be served hot or cold. An older baby would probably eat a mashed up portion of the loaf. For younger babies (eight to twelve months), to avoid giving them egg, put aside a spoonful or two of the cooked lentil and vegetable mixture before the egg, sesame seed and seasoning are added.

*This recipe is suitable for freezing.

SERVES 4

---

1 tablespoon oil
1 onion, peeled and finely chopped
2 leeks, trimmed and chopped
2 parsnips, peeled and diced
2 carrots, peeled and diced
175 g (6 oz) red lentils, washed
1 teaspoon chopped fresh thyme
1 teaspoon made mild mustard
450 ml (³/₄ pint) water
Seasoning
2 eggs, beaten
2 tablespoons ground sesame seeds
1 tablespoon whole sesame seeds

Pre-heat the oven to gas mark 5, 190°C (375°F).

Heat the oil and gently fry the onion and leeks until soft, adding a little more oil if necessary. Add the vegetables and lentils, stir well and cook for 3 to 4 minutes. Add the thyme and mustard then pour over the water. Bring to the boil, cover and simmer until the lentils are well cooked and most of the water has been absorbed. This takes 20 to 25 minutes. Leave to cool slightly then season to taste. Add the beaten eggs and ground sesame seeds. Spoon into an oiled shallow baking dish or loaf tin. Sprinkle with the remaining sesame seeds and bake in the oven for 35 to 40 minutes or until quite firm. Serve hot with tomato sauce or ketchup.

•

Red Cabbage with Walnuts and Soured Cream

This is a useful slow-cooking vegetable dish which can accompany other recipes such as aduki burgers, lentil and sesame bake or just a baked potato. The nuts and cream add useful nutrients if you wish to eat it as a snack. It tastes good hot or cold. Surprisingly, this dish may be enjoyed by your baby after eight months or so. Be sure to remove all the pieces of nut and break down the sultanas or they will go straight through.

This recipe is suitable for freezing without the soured cream.

SERVES 4

2 tablespoons oil
1 onion, peeled and chopped
750 g (1¹/₂ lb) red cabbage, finely sliced
350 g (12 oz) cooking apples peeled, cored and chopped
75 g (3 oz) sultanas
50 g (2 oz) walnut pieces
1 tablespoon concentrated apple juice
1 tablespoon red wine vinegar
6 tablespoons stock or water
Seasoning
150 ml (5 fl oz) soured cream
Juice of ¹/₂ lemon

Heat the oil and gently fry the onion until soft. Add the red cabbage and cook for 5 minutes, stirring well, then add the apples, sultanas and walnut pieces. Pour over the concentrated apple juice, wine vinegar and stock or water. Cover the pan and simmer gently for 1 to 1¹/₂ hours or until the cabbage is very soft. Add a little more liquid if necessary. Season to taste. Mix the soured cream and lemon juice and beat until thick. Serve this with the red cabbage.

•

Ratatouille with Tofu

Ratatouille is a classic dish which can be made with a variety of vegetables including aubergine, courgettes, peppers and mushrooms. It is excellent with tofu which soaks up the flavours of the sauce and also adds extra nutritional value. Babies of eight months upwards can eat portions of this dish chopped finely or mashed.

This recipe is suitable for freezing without the tofu or pesto. These can be added once the mixture has been defrosted.

SERVES 4

2–3 tablespoons olive oil
1 onion, peeled and finely chopped
1–2 cloves garlic, peeled and crushed
1 aubergine, diced
1 × 350 g (12 oz) packet firm tofu, cut into chunks
1 red pepper, de-seeded and diced
4 medium courgettes, chopped
1 × 500 g (1 lb 2 oz) packet creamed tomatoes
1 teaspoon marjoram
1 bay leaf
1 tablespoon pesto sauce
150 ml (5 fl oz) stock
Seasoning

Heat the oil and gently fry the onion and garlic until soft. Add the aubergine and fry until quite soft, adding more oil if necessary. Add the tofu, mixing it in carefully, then add the other vegetables and cook for a few minutes. Pour over the creamed tomatoes and add the herbs and pesto sauce. Bring the mixture to the boil, cover and simmer for 30 to 40 minutes, adding just enough stock to keep the ratatouille moist. Remove the bay leaf. Season to taste and serve hot with pasta or baked potatoes.

•

Spicy Vegetables

This quick spiced vegetable dish has a creamy texture thanks to the combination of aubergine and yoghurt. As the spices are quite mild, it is suitable for an older child, around a year, but you must make sure you remove all the pieces of almond. Add a few ground almonds instead or mash a little nut butter with the rice.

This recipe is not suitable for freezing.

SERVES 4

2–3 tablespoons oil
1 onion, peeled and chopped
1 aubergine, diced
1/2 teaspoon cumin seeds
1/2 teaspoon turmeric
1/2 teaspoon garam masala
150 ml (5 fl oz) natural yoghurt
1 teaspoon wholewheat flour
1 red pepper, de-seeded and chopped
225 g (8 oz) broccoli florets
50 g (2 oz) peas
25g (1 oz) blanched split almonds
150 ml (5 fl oz) stock or water
1 tablespoon tomato purée
Seasoning

Heat the oil and gently fry the onion until soft. Add the aubergine and cumin seeds and cook until soft, adding more oil if necessary. Mix the powdered spices with a little water then add these to the pan with the yoghurt and flour. Stir well and cook for a few minutes. Add the remaining vegetables and nuts. Cook for a few minutes, then pour over the stock or water and stir in the tomato purée. Bring to the boil then cover and simmer for 20 to 25 minutes until the vegetables are tender. Season to taste. Serve with rice or bread.

•

Vegetable Bake

Eggs, well cooked, can be a nutritious addition to your diet. In this recipe they are combined with a mixture of vegetables and crème fraîche which adds a rich creamy flavour. Serve this as a light supper or as a substantial breakfast or brunch dish. This recipe is only suitable for older babies (over one year) once you have established that they will have no adverse reaction to eggs.

This recipe is not suitable for freezing.

SERVES 4

2 tablespoons olive oil
1 onion, peeled and chopped
1 clove garlic, peeled and crushed
225 g (8 oz) courgettes, diced
1 red pepper, de-seeded and chopped
1 green pepper, de-seeded and chopped
225 g (8 oz) mushrooms
1 teaspoon marjoram
3 eggs
175 ml (6 fl oz) crème fraîche
Seasoning

Pre-heat the oven to gas mark 4, 180°C (350°F).

Heat the oil and fry the onion and garlic until soft, then add the courgettes, peppers and mushrooms. Stir well and cook for 10 minutes. Remove from the heat and sprinkle over the marjoram. Beat the eggs and crème fraîche, pour over the vegetable mixture and season to taste. Spoon into a well greased ovenproof dish and bake in the oven for 35 minutes. Serve hot.

•

Vegetables with Millet

This is a recipe rather like a risotto which can be made with various combinations of vegetables. It is important to cook the millet thoroughly so that it gains a creamy texture otherwise the end result can taste dry. Adapt this recipe for your baby by removing some of the cooked mixture before adding the sunflower seeds. Add a little extra water or milk and mash to a suitable consistency.

This recipe is suitable for freezing.

SERVES 4

1 tablespoon oil
1 onion, peeled and chopped
2 peppers, de-seeded and chopped
1 carrot, peeled and chopped
225 g (8 oz) mushrooms, chopped
225 g (8 oz) millet
750 ml (1¹/₄ pints) water
2 tablespoons chopped fresh parsley
1 tablespoon tomato purée
50 g (2 oz) sunflower seeds
1–2 tablespoons shoyu
Seasoning

Heat the oil and gently fry the onion until soft. Then add the vegetables and cook until they start to soften. Stir in the millet then pour over the water. Mix in the parsley and tomato purée. Bring to the boil, then cover the pan and simmer for 25 to 30 minutes, stirring occasionally and adding extra liquid if necessary.

Meanwhile toast the sunflower seeds for 5 minutes in a hot oven or 2 minutes in a microwave. Pour over the shoyu and toast again for 3 minutes in the oven or 1 minute in a microwave. Stir the sunflower seeds into the cooked millet and season to taste.

•

LIGHT MEALS AND SNACKS

At various times during your pregnancy and afterwards, you may find you would prefer to eat snacks and lighter meals rather than more substantial food. It could be that your stomach simply hasn't got the room for too many big meals. It might be that when you are on your own, during the day for example, it is too much effort to cook food for one. After the baby is born, you may find it difficult to find time to do much cooking. In the following sections I've given several suggestions as to how to prepare quick simple meals. These are not so much recipes as ideas using combinations of food that I hope will appeal and perhaps inspire you, too. My suggestions are a stage more complicated than simply putting a piece of cheese between two slices of bread but I think that a few extra ingredients and a little time produces more interesting meals which should encourage you to eat well.

Baked Potatoes

Baked potatoes are useful both as part of a meal or as a substantial snack on their own. Once you have introduced your baby to solids, he may well enjoy the inside of a baked potato mashed with vegetables, cottage cheese, grated cheese or tofu.

Baked potatoes needn't be smothered in butter, but can be served in a number of ways. I've included recipes for ratatouille and tofu as well as red cabbage and walnuts that go well with potatoes. For simpler snacks try some of the following ideas:

- tofu mashed with enough pesto sauce to suit your taste;
- cottage cheese mixed with chopped nuts and parsley;
- mashed avocado with yoghurt, walnut pieces and diced apple;
- finely grated carrot and chopped dates mixed with fromage frais and poppy seeds;
- ground almonds blended with tomatoes and a little vinegar then mixed with olive oil to a creamy consistency;
- red kidney beans mixed with chopped onion, parsley and a few drops of tabasco sauce;
- baked beans with grated apple;

- finely grated carrot and cabbage mixed with yoghurt, flavoured with mustard and topped with toasted sunflower seeds;
- silken tofu with shoyu and garlic, plus a little lemon juice to taste;
- frozen peas cooked then puréed with cream cheese or fromage frais and mint.

Sandwiches, Baguettes, Rolls and Pitta Pockets

There is more to a sandwich than plain sliced bread. Not only can you get a good variety of flavoured breads – rye, oatmeal, mixed seed and pumpernickel, for example – but you can also get plenty of different shapes to keep your meals interesting. There is no end to the choice of nutritious fillings: nut butters, cheeses, beans, pâtés and tofu are just the beginning. Add some salad ingredients to get extra nutrients and a variety of textures. Here are a few ideas:

- slices of avocado with alfalfa sprouts and tomato sprinkled with olive oil and black pepper;
- slices of smoked tofu with finely chopped onion and watercress;
- thin slices of raw mushroom and cucumber and shredded spinach topped with crème fraîche;
- tahini mixed with olive oil, lemon juice and shoyu topped with bean sprouts and shredded Chinese leaves;
- cottage cheese with chopped apricots and toasted sunflower seeds;
- cooked red lentils mixed with peanut butter and mango chutney with finely chopped peppers;
- goats' cheese and mixed salad leaves (radicchio, lollo rosso and cos);
- mashed chick peas with tahini, lemon juice and olive oil with olives and cucumber;
- cream cheese with chopped celery, toasted almonds and raisins;
- sliced Italian tomatoes with pesto and black pepper.

Salads

At times when you don't feel hungry it is good to eat salads which can give you useful vitamins and minerals. Adding ingredients such as nuts, seeds, dairy products or cooked pulses and grains can turn salads into a fully fledged meal. Even if you can't be bothered to chop anything, a plate of whole tomatoes, sticks of celery, crunchy lettuce leaves and button mushrooms served with bread, chunks of cheese or a substantial nut dressing can make the basis of a healthy meal.
Tips to remember about salads are:
- salad ingredients should be stored in the refrigerator
- always wash the ingredients really well
- try to prepare them just before you are ready to eat
- try to include some dark leafy ingredients such as water-cress, broccoli, or spinach. If you are not so keen on the latter raw, lightly steam them first then marinade in a dressing and leave to cool
- dried fruits go well with many salads adding extra vitamins and minerals (particularly iron) as well as calories.

Dressings

It is unwise to eat home-made mayonnaise when you are pregnant but there are plenty of alternatives:
- use natural yoghurt flavoured with herbs, mustard or roasted seeds such as cumin; use on its own or mix with a cottage or cream cheese or mashed avocado
- make a more substantial French dressing by adding ground nuts to the mixture and a matching oil (walnuts and walnut oil, hazelnuts and hazelnut oil)
- Silken tofu blends easily to a cream. Make this savoury with shoyu, garlic and tahini, or sweeten with fruit juices

Stir-Fry

Your image of stir-fry may be that it does involve a good deal of preparation. Really it is no more than getting a salad ready. Once the ingredients are chopped, they take little time to cook. Producing a stir-fry is an excellent way of keeping up the amount of vegetables you eat, which is helpful from the nutritional point of view. In practical terms they are also a good device for using up little bits of vegetables all too often at the back of the fridge. This seems to be the state of most post-pregnant refrigerators!

There is no special skill in producing a stir-fry, but I hope you find the following tips useful

- get everything chopped first so you can concentrate on the cooking once you start
- chop things even-sized if possible so things cook at roughly the same time
- use as large a pan as possible if you don't have a wok
- put in the longest cooking items first (carrots before mushrooms)
- add a little liquid at the end of cooking and put on the lid for a couple of minutes if you prefer a soft texture to your vegetables. You can just use stock, shoyu, fruit juices, particularly orange or lemon, or mixtures of these
- use stir-fry as an accompaniment to a meal
- if serving on its own, have rice or noodles and a handful of bean sprouts, toasted nuts and seeds or chunks of tofu to add to the nutritional value.

Puddings and Cakes

It is useful to have some quick and simple puddings and cake recipes to stave off hunger pangs and satisfy sweet cravings that you may have during and after pregnancy. Most of the recipes given here do contain some sugar but probably less than would be used in many commercial products. Extra sweetening comes from dried fruits and honey which are useful nutritious ingredients. It is probably true that most of these recipes would be eaten by an older baby, but whether you give him a taste is up to you.

Carrot and Sultana Cake

This is a quick moist cake, useful as a morning or afternoon snack or even pudding, perhaps with yoghurt or fromage frais.
  *This recipe is suitable for freezing

MAKES 1 × 900 G (2 LB) CAKE

100 g (4 oz) sultanas
50 g (2 oz) apricots, chopped
50 ml (2 fl oz) orange juice
100 g (4 oz) butter or margarine
100 g (4 oz) honey
50 g (2 oz) sugar
225 g (8 oz) wholewheat flour
2 teaspoons cinnamon
2 teaspoons baking powder
225 g (8 oz) carrots, peeled and grated

Soak the sultanas and apricots in the orange juice for at least 30 minutes. Pre-heat the oven to gas mark 3, 160°C (325°F).
  Melt the butter or margarine with the honey and sugar. Mix the flour with the spice and baking powder, then pour over the melted margarine and mix well. Add the carrots and the soaked sultanas and apricots and mix well. Spoon the mixture into a well greased 900 g (2 lb) loaf tin. Bake in the oven for 60 to 70 minutes, or until firm to the touch, and a skewer inserted in the centre comes out clean.   •

Giant Cheese Scone

Scones make a good snack any time of day. I've given a savoury version here to contrast with the sweet cakes and biscuits in the rest of this section. Making the scone in one large round saves you the effort of cutting the dough. It also means you get it in the oven more quickly which should create a better result.

*This recipe is suitable for freezing.

SERVES 4

225 g (8 oz) wholewheat flour
1 tablespoon baking powder
A pinch of salt
A pinch of paprika
A pinch of mustard powder
25 g (1 oz) butter or margarine
100 g (4 oz) Cheddar cheese, finely grated
1 egg
150 ml (5 fl oz) milk

Pre-heat the oven to gas mark 6, 200°C (400°F).

Mix the flour with the baking powder, salt and spices. Rub in the butter or margarine until the mixture resembles fine bread-crumbs. Mix in the cheese, saving a little to put on the top. Beat the egg and add enough milk to make up to 150 ml (5 fl oz). Pour enough of this mixture over the flour to give a soft dough. Turn on to a lightly floured board and knead lightly. Shape into one large round about 1 cm (½ in) thick. Mark lightly into 8 portions, then scatter the remaining cheese over the top. Bake in the oven for 20 minutes. Leave to cool on a wire rack.

•

Mixed Fruit Loaf

This is an easy loaf, made in just two stages. All you have to remember is to soak the fruit well in advance. Use concentrated apple juice (diluted about 1:10) to make the apple juice. Use this loaf as a mid-morning or tea time snack. It is delicious toasted and spread with a little butter or margarine.

*This recipe is suitable for freezing.

MAKES 1 × 900 G (2 LB) LOAF

---

175 g (6 oz) sultanas
175 g (6 oz) raisins
50 g (2 oz) dark brown sugar
300 ml (10 fl oz) hot apple juice
1 egg
275 g (10 oz) wholewheat flour
2 teaspoons baking powder

Put the sultanas and raisins into a large bowl. Dissolve the sugar in the hot apple juice then pour over the dried fruit. Cover and leave to soak for 3 to 4 hours.

Pre-heat the oven to gas mark 5, 190°C (375°F).

Mix the egg into the fruit, then add the flour and baking powder and mix thoroughly. Spoon the mixture into a greased 900 g (2 lb) loaf tin. Bake in the oven for 45 to 50 minutes. To tell if the loaf is cooked, insert a skewer and check that it comes out clean.

•

Muesli Biscuits

This is a very simple recipe for crunchy home-made biscuits which will be much in demand from visiting parents and possibly their babies.

*This recipe is suitable for freezing

MAKES ABOUT 24 BISCUITS

100 g (4 oz) butter or margarine
50 g (2 oz) soft brown sugar
100 g (4 oz) wholewheat flour
100 g (4 oz) muesli, muesli base or porridge oats

Pre-heat the oven to gas mark 4, 180°C (350°F).

Cream the butter or margarine and sugar together until light and fluffy. Add the flour and muesli and cream again until the mixture forms a firm dough. Using a lightly floured board, roll or press out the dough to about 1 cm (½ in) thick. Cut into rounds with a small sized cutter and place on a greased baking sheet. Bake in the oven for 15 to 18 minutes or until just brown. Leave to cool on a wire rack.

•

Prune Purée with Fromage Frais

This is a very simple recipe which may tempt you to eat prunes if you need to. It is also delicious as a quick pudding, and without the orange rind might be enjoyed by your baby.

This recipe is not suitable for freezing

SERVES 4

175 g (6 oz) prunes
300 ml (10 fl oz) orange juice
1 teaspoon grated orange rind
225 g (8 oz) fromage frais

Soak the prunes in the orange juice and rind for several hours, then bring to the boil and cook for 20 minutes or until soft, adding more water if necessary. Drain and remove the stones. Using a food processor, purée the prunes with the fromage frais until smooth. Serve chilled.

•

Sticky Fruit Pudding

This is a hefty steamed pudding that should certainly fill any post-natal tummy.

This recipe is not suitable for freezing.

SERVES 4

175 g (6 oz) wholewheat flour
1 teaspoon baking powder
1 egg, beaten
120 ml (4 fl oz) milk
50 g (2 oz) soft brown sugar
175 g (6 oz) butter or margarine
225 g (8 oz) mixed dates and figs, chopped
175 g (6 oz) sugar-free apricot jam

Mix the flour with the baking powder. Beat the egg with the milk. Cream together the sugar and butter or margarine until light and fluffy, then add the flour and egg-milk mixture alternately, beating vigorously. Stir in the dried fruit and apricot jam. Spoon the mixture into a greased 1.2 litre (2 pint) pudding basin, cover with foil and steam for 1½ to 2 hours, topping up with boiling water as necessary. Alternatively put in a dish suitable for the microwave, cover with microwave cling film, pierce a few times and cook for 8 to 10 minutes. Leave to stand for several minutes. Test with a skewer which should come out clean when inserted if the pudding is cooked.

•

Drinks

Pregnancy makes you thirstier. It is important that you drink plenty not just to satisfy your thirst but also to help relieve conditions such as constipation. You may go off caffeine drinks such as tea and coffee and you may also want to avoid heavily sugared drinks such as squashes or fizzy drinks. There are all sorts of alternatives.

In this section I've given recipes for drinks that are almost a meal in themselves as well as some suggestions for soft drinks to quench your thirst and act as an alternative to alcohol. As for alternatives to caffeine drinks, there is now a huge range of herbal teas, decaffeinated tea and coffee as well as grain coffee (usually based on barley), carob drinks and malted drinks made with hot water.

Mini-Meals

The following recipes are all virtually mini-meals which act as a snack or as a good source of nutrients at times when you can't face a full meal. The yoghurt and tofu are interchangeable if you prefer one rather than another. Make these 'drinks' just before eating as they are best when freshly prepared.

Good Morning Yoghurt

SERVES 1

25 g (1 oz) sultanas
5 tablespoons orange juice or orange juice diluted with mineral water
150 ml (5 fl oz) natural yoghurt
2 tablespoons wheatgerm
Honey and cinnamon to taste

Soak the sultanas in the juice for 2 hours or use a microwave to plump them up. Then purée them with the remaining ingredients until quite smooth. Add honey to taste. Pour the mixture into a large glass and decorate with a little cinnamon.

Silken Tofu Pick-Me-Up

SERVES 1

150 g (5 oz) silken tofu
1 small banana
Juice of 1/2 orange
1 tablespoon granola

Blend the tofu with the banana and orange juice. Pour into a glass and sprinkle over the granola.

Pear and Vanilla Cream

SERVES 1

150 g (5 oz) silken tofu
1 ripe pear, peeled, cored and chopped
2–3 drops of vanilla essence
Honey to taste

Purée all the ingredients until thoroughly smooth. Adjust the sweetening to taste.

Almond and Sesame Milk

SERVES 1

25 g (1 oz) ground almonds
120 ml (4 fl oz) water
2 teaspoons tahini
Honey or malt extract to taste

Blend the almonds with the water until quite smooth. Add the tahini and sweetening and blend again thoroughly. If you prefer the mixture to be thicker, add extra tahini.

Californian Smoothie

Smoothies are from the United States and are usually blended mixtures of fruits with or without fruit juices or mineral water. You can use different combinations of all sorts of fruit, depending on what is in season. I find adding a banana or mango gives the dish a pleasant creamy texture.

SERVES 1

Juice of 1 large orange
Juice of $^1/_2$ grapefruit
1 banana
Freshly grated nutmeg

Blend the fruit juices with the banana until completely smooth. Pour into a glass and top with grated nutmeg.

Alternatives to Alcohol

Look out for the varieties of concentrated fruit juices on sale, such as apple, pear or combinations of fruits such as apple and cherry. These can be diluted with plain water, sparkling water or with other fresh juices to produce a punch. There are also plenty of flavoured carbonated waters with ginseng and other exotic ingredients which make an excellent alternative to wine. Old-fashioned lemonade has become more popular recently. It is quite easy to make your own. This is one occasion where I use white sugar as I find brown sugar makes the end result murky.

Home Made Lemonade

MAKES ABOUT 1.2 LITRES (2 PINTS)

3 lemons, well scrubbed
100 g (4 oz) caster sugar
600 ml (1 pint) boiling water
600 ml (1 pint) carbonated water

Halve the lemons and squeeze out the juice. (If you put them first in the microwave for a few seconds you get more juice.) Put the juice and lemon halves in a bowl with the sugar. Add the boiling water and stir until the sugar dissolves. Leave to cool. Strain through a fine sieve. Just before serving, dilute with sparkling water.

Breakfast

Try not to skip breakfast as it will give you energy for the day ahead. A good cereal and bread or toast with fruit juice, fresh fruit or a fruit compote doesn't take much trouble to prepare. If you have time to cook there are lots of ideas such as beans or scrambled tofu on toast or the vegetable bake in the main course section for something more elaborate.

Twenty-Four Hour Muesli

This recipe doesn't take that long to prepare – it is soaked overnight which gives the finished dish a creamy texture.

SERVES 1

4 tablespoons porridge oats
4 tablespoons mineral water
2 teaspoons honey
1 teaspoon grated orange rind
4 tablespoons fromage frais
1 apple, peeled and finely grated
Selection of chopped fresh fruit, toasted almond flakes
(optional)

Soak the oats in the water and stir in the honey and orange rind. Leave to stand overnight.

The next day, stir in the fromage frais and grated apple. Add extra chopped fresh fruit and toasted nuts if you wish.

Millet Porridge

This is especially easy to make with flakes rather than whole grains.

SERVES 1

1 small cup millet flakes
2¹/₂–3 cups soya milk or water

Stir the flakes into the milk or water and bring to the boil. Simmer for 4 to 5 minutes, stirring continuously until the mixture is creamy and the flakes are cooked. Add more liquid if necessary.

Spiced Fruit Compote

Dried fruit dishes can be a delicious addition to any breakfast spread. Apart from their nutritional benefit, they can be prepared well in advance in large quantities and will keep (and improve) in the fridge for several days.

SERVES 4

225 g (8 oz) mixed dried fruit salad (prunes, figs,
apricots, apples)
300 ml (¹/₂ pint) water
2 tablespoons concentrated apple or grape juice
4 cloves
1 cinnamon stick or piece of peeled fresh root ginger

Soak the fruit overnight in water and apple juice. Add the spices and gently poach the fruit in its soaking liquid for 30 to 40 minutes. Remove the spices. Serve hot or cold.

Hunza Apricots

Hunza apricots are small whole apricots usually sold complete with the stone. They come from an area of the world whose population has a reputation for longevity said to be thanks to their diet of these apricots and yoghurt.

SERVES 4

225 g (8 oz) hunza apricots

Wash the apricots in water to remove any dust. Soak them in fresh water for several hours. Once plump they are ready to eat. If you prefer a softer texture and a thicker juice, bring the apricots to the boil and gently simmer for 25 to 30 minutes. Serve hot or cold.

Useful Addresses

VEGETARIAN, VEGAN AND ENVIRONMENTAL ISSUES

- **The Vegetarian Society**
Parkdale
Dunham Road
Altrincham,
Cheshire WA14 4QG
061–928 0793

Gives information on all aspects of vegetarianism. Extensive publication list including nutritional and practical advice for feeding babies and children.

- **The Vegan Society**
7 Battle Road
St Leonards-on-Sea
East Sussex TN37 7AA
0424–427393

Gives information and nutritional advice on being vegan. Publication list.

- **The Women's Environmental Network**
Aberdeen Studios
22 Highbury Grove
London N5 2EA
071–354 8823

Runs campaigns on environmental issues specifically affecting women such as sanitary protection and nappies and the environment.

CHILDBIRTH AND MATERNITY

- **Active Birth Centre**
55 Dartmouth Park Road
London NW5 1SL
071–267 3006

A London based organisation with teachers throughout the United Kingdom. Combination of information and physical practice of yoga help women take more responsibility for childbirth.

- **National Childbirth Trust**
  Alexandra House
  Oldham Terrace
  Acton
  London W3 6NH
  081–992 8637
Offers information and support on all aspects of pregnancy, childbirth, childcare and early parenthood. Extensive publication list and sales of maternity related products.

- **The Maternity Alliance**
  15 Britannia Street
  London WC1X 9JP
  071–837 1265
Campaigns for improvements in maternity care.

- **Society to Support Home Confinement**
  Lydgate Lane
  Wolsingham
  Bishop Auckland DL13 3HA
  0388–528 044

BREAST FEEDING

- **The National Childbirth Trust** (see above)

- **La Leche League**
  BM 3424
  London WC1N 3XX
  071–404 5011
Offers information and encouragement for those who want to breast feed

ALTERNATIVE TREATMENTS

- **Active Birth Centre** (see above)

- **Ann Lett School of Reflex Zone Therapy**
  87 Oakington Avenue
  Wembley Park
  London HA9 8HY
  081–908 2201

- **Association of Reflexologists**
  27 Old Gloucester Street
  London WC1 3XX
  081–445 0154

- **British Acupuncture Association and Register**
  34 Alderney Street
  London SW1V 4EU
  071–834 1012

- **British Homoeopathic Association**
  27a Devonshire Street
  London W1N 1RJ
  071–935 2163

- **Healing Herbs**
  PO Box 65
  Hereford HR2 0UW

- **The International Federation of Aromatherapists**
  4 East Mearn Road
  Dulwich
  London SE21 8HA

- **Raymar (TNS)**
  PO Box 16
  Fairview Estate
  Reading Road
  Henley-on Thames RG9 1LL
  0491 578446

- **The Register of Traditional Chinese Medicine**
  19 Trinity Road
  London N2 8JJ
  081–883 8431

- **The General Council and Register of Osteopaths**
  56 London Steet
  Reading
  Berkshire RG1 480
  0734–576585/260

EXERCISE

- **The Sports Council**
  16 Upper Woburn Place
  London WC1H 0QP
  071–388 1277

Index